ESSEX FROM THE A

Archaeology and history from aerial photographs
by David Strachan

© *Essex County Council 1998*
Michael Burchell BA MA MRTPI
Head of Planning
County Hall, Chelmsford CM1 1LF

ISBN (1 85281 165 X)

Site Locations

Contents

Foreword

The Archaeology Section of Essex County Council was established within the Planning Department in 1972. It carries out a wide range of work, including excavation and recording prior to development, research projects, conservation management and administration of the Sites and Monuments Record, which contains details of all known archaeological sites, many of which were first discovered from the air.

This publication, dealing with the changing nature of the landscape, is timely for a number of reasons. The end of the millennium will mark the conclusion of a century which has seen unprecedented human impact on the natural environment. Attitudes and approaches to conservation and management have changed in recent years as a result. Policy and practice, from a national level to the site specific, now concentrates on sustainability based upon an inter-disciplinary approach. Aerial photography, containing a wealth of information about both past and present environments, plays a key role in the study of both natural and 'built' environments. As a result, it can be used to development strategies for present management, while offering a record of the existing landscape for future generations to study. Administratively, it is a time of change for the county of Essex, as both Southend and Thurrock districts became new Unitary Authorities in 1998.

This volume draws from a variety of sources, including collections at Cambridge University and the Royal Commission on the Historical Monuments of England, who have funded much of the air photographic work in recent years. The majority of images, however, were taken as part of the ongoing survey carried out by members of the Archaeology Section. Many of these were taken in the exceptional summers of 1995 and 1996, when near drought conditions resulted in the widespread appearance of the 'cropmark' phenomenon. The aerial view is usually engaging and often striking, and the images contained within show many places of interest to visit in the county. A visit to the remarkable barns at Cressing Temple, or the impressive fort at Tilbury, will be greatly enhanced with the aid of the aerial photographs contained in this volume. The book is ideally suited for the armchair archaeologist and landscape historian, since it offers an exciting and visually stimulating aerial tour of Essex though the last 5,000 years of its history. I commend this volume, and congratulate the Archaeology Section on its preparation and publication.

Chris Manning-Press

Councillor C. Manning-Press
Chair of the Heritage, Leisure and Culture Board, Essex County Council

Introduction: Why Aerial Photography in Archaeology?

The aerial view

Aerial photographs provide us with images of the landscape around us which are simultaneously striking and informative. As a result, in addition to their use as an illustrative medium, aerial photographs are studied by a variety of people for many different reasons. Cartographers, civil engineers, geologists, and lawyers are among those who regularly use aerial photographs as a source of information for their own interests. Interpreted by archaeologists and historians, aerial photographs can reveal the evolution of the physical remains of past human activity.

Since the earliest farmers of the prehistoric era, over five thousand years ago, people have built set-tlements, constructed trackways and roads, cultivated crops, domesticated animals, buried their dead, and built structures where they could congregate for worship. The remains of these structures can, over the subsequent centuries, become incorporated into the evolving landscape. It is often possible to view the remains of these past structures from the air, and photographs provide an ideal method of recording their size, shape, and position in the landscape.

During a flight over the Essex landscape, an archaeologist will be continually reminded of the distant past by views of churches, occasional castles and moated sites of the Middle Ages, and indeed, by buildings, roads and field boundaries of our more recent past. During the early summer,

however, when the crops in arable fields begin to ripen, features of buried ancient landscapes can become visible as patterns in the crops; a phenomenon known as cropmarks. The crops respond to variations of water and nutrients below the land surface, showing the outline of buried structures. The cropmarks last only a few weeks, sometimes only days, but they offer the archaeologist a unique opportunity to discover new sites and study them without excavation. The aerial perspective is the only way to record these archaeological sites, of which no trace exists above the ground.

Indeed, it will become evident that the photographs within represent composite images of the remnants of a number of landscapes which have changed and developed over very long periods of time. For example, the buried remains of a prehistoric domestic enclosure may be viewed as a cropmark in an arable field beside a church of Medieval date which has a road, of much later date, passing nearby. In many instances, each successive development will represent little or no continuity of function from one period to the next. In other examples, however, such as a Roman fort which dictates the layout of a Medieval town and subsequent city, there may be a high level of continuity in the form of orientation and layout over time. By interpreting the nature of individual built components of the landscape, the archaeologist hopes to understand the developments which have taken place in the way people have lived and used the land from the earliest farmers until the recent past.

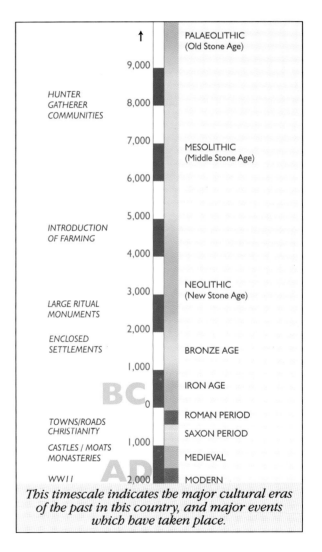

	↑	PALAEOLITHIC (Old Stone Age)
	9,000	
HUNTER GATHERER COMMUNITIES	8,000	
	7,000	MESOLITHIC (Middle Stone Age)
	6,000	
INTRODUCTION OF FARMING	5,000	
	4,000	
LARGE RITUAL MONUMENTS	3,000	NEOLITHIC (New Stone Age)
	2,000	
ENCLOSED SETTLEMENTS		BRONZE AGE
	1,000	
	BC 0	IRON AGE
TOWNS/ROADS CHRISTIANITY		ROMAN PERIOD
		SAXON PERIOD
CASTLES / MOATS MONASTERIES	1,000	
	AD	MEDIEVAL
WWII	2,000	MODERN

This timescale indicates the major cultural eras of the past in this country, and major events which have taken place.

The Development of Aerial Archaeology

In 1858, Gaspard Felix Tournachon, known as Nadar, took aerial photographs from a captive balloon, having already applied for a patent on the idea of using the photographs for the production of maps. Henry Negretti took the first recorded aerial photographs of Britain in 1863, during a balloon flight over London. The military potential of aviation was soon recognised, however, and this resulted in many technical improvements related to flying. The first aerial photograph of Stonehenge was taken from a military balloon in 1906, and archaeologists began to realise the potential of aerial photography during these early days of flight. The 1914-18 war saw considerable developments in aviation and produced the pioneers of·aerial archaeology, such as O.G.S. Crawford and G.W.G. Allen, who were among the first individuals to regularly record archaeological sites from aircraft. The early photographers used hand-held cameras and simply took 'oblique' photographs, at an angle from the aircraft. While this type of photography results in distortion of features caused by perspective, it is still regularly employed by archaeologists as it is flexible and cost efficient. The Second World War also saw great advances in terms of aircraft, camera, and film technology. The RAF developed the use of 'vertical' photography, which results in what amounts to photographic maps of large blocks of the landscape. This is achieved by mounting cameras, which point directly down to the earth, onto an aircraft and taking a series of overlapping images at regular intervals. This technique also allows any specific image on a flight path to be viewed stereo-scopically, giving a 'pop-up', three-dimensional view of the landscape. While this technique was developed for reconnaissance over enemy territory during the war, the RAF subsequently photographed almost all of the country in the immediate post-war period as part of their National Survey. The survey created what is effectively a 'snap-shot' photographic Domesday Book of the country in 1946. The photographs taken during this, and subsequent surveys, offer a unique and valuable resource which records the evolving landscape of the country in the early post-war era.

In 1945, J.K.S. St Joseph, who was then a lecturer in Geology, began a programme of aerial reconnaissance for Cambridge University, which was to result in the establishment of the Cambridge University Committee for Aerial Photography (CUCAP). The survey was multi-disciplinary in nature, recording natural landscapes as well as archaeological and historical sites. The CUCAP collection now contains over 400,000 photographs of the British Isles, Ireland and parts of the continent. Many of the cropmark sites in Essex were discovered by CUCAP during regular flights over the county between the 1950s and 1970s.

The Royal Commission on the Historical Monuments of England (RCHME) curates a national record of information, in various forms, relating to ancient monuments and historic buildings in its National Monuments Record (NMR). The NMR contains a collection of around 3,000,000 individual vertical aerial photographs and some 600,000 oblique photographs which cover all of England. The vertical collection consists of material taken by the RAF, the Ordnance Survey and various commercial companies, while the specialist oblique photography, which embraces archaeological, architectural and landscape subjects, results from the work of the RCHMEs ongoing programme of reconnaissance and various regional aerial photographers. The collection is held at the National Monuments Record Centre in Swindon.

While both CUCAP and the RCHME have carried out reconnaissance in order to record both upstanding architectural monuments and cropmark sites over Essex, a number of local archaeologists, notably Ida McMaster and Captain R. H. Farrands, have also flown for this purpose. In addition, in the 1970s, the then county archaeologist J. Hedges began to carry out occasional sorties in order to record cropmarks and excavations. This led to the establishment of a regular programme of annual reconnaissance in the 1980s. Many of the photographs reproduced here result from aerial survey partly funded by the RCMHE, carried out by the Archaeology Section of Essex County Council.

The development of satellite imagery over the last few decades, indicates the enormous technological leaps which have occurred since the early balloon photography carried out only a hundred and fifty years ago. It also attests, however, the continued desire to witness the earth from the aerial perspective, allowing us not only the ability to record the current state of affairs, but to monitor change over time.

Below left:
The site as it appeared in 1961 with the topsoil around enclosure (D) removed. Gravel extraction, visible to the south of the road, was to extend into the area of the cropmark complex and destroy the archaeology. The buried archaeological features, which caused the cropmarks, are visible as marks in the sub-soil.

Below centre:
Archaeologists have began to study the features by cutting trenches across them and recording in detail the layout of structures and the position and nature of small finds. This information is then used to assign a date and function to the individual structures, which allows the development of the area over time to be understood.

Excavating the cropmark complex at Mucking, Thurrock

The multi-period cropmark complex at Mucking as it appeared in 1957. The Bronze Age enclosure (A) and Iron Age enclosures (B) are the main features visible. The graves of a Romano-British cemetery also appear as elongated dots inside enclosure (C) and many of the larger dots around A and B are the remains of Saxon sunken-featured buildings.

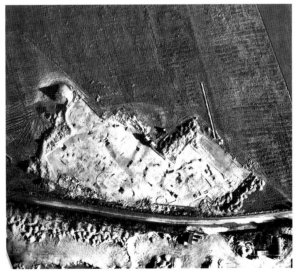

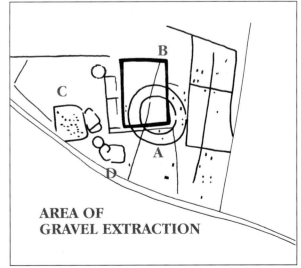

AREA OF GRAVEL EXTRACTION

Cropmark Archaeology - recording hidden landscapes

The remains of past human activity can be seen from the air in a number of ways. In addition to churches, castles and other old buildings, partly eroded remains of past structures, in the form of earthen mounds and banks can also be viewed. These sites are known as 'earthworks'. More elusive, however, are the remains of buried archaeological sites which, in certain conditions, are best viewed from above. When arable fields are ploughed, it is often possible to view the flattened remains of old buildings, roads and field boundaries because of the difference in the soils and materials which make up the remains. For example, the site of a demolished house might be recognisable from the air due to the concentration of brick, tile and other debris which is visible because of variations of colour and texture. These sites are known as 'soilmarks'. In recent years, pioneering work in Essex has helped develop the use of aerial photography along the coast, and in particular on the extensive inter-tidal mudflats. Flying along the coast at low tide, timber fish weirs, oyster pits, ship-wrecks and hulks of other old boats have been recorded in this way. Many of these areas are extremely inaccessible, and aerial photography allows archaeologists to rapidly cover large areas and locate structures which they can then visit on foot.

Perhaps the most remarkable type of site, however, are those known as 'cropmarks'. In this instance, variations in the sub-soil caused by buried archaeo-logical features results in differential crop growth. In early summer, as crops begin to ripen, the ditches, walls and pits of past settlements, fields and places of worship affect the rate at which the crops change colour, and the speed and height to which they grow. For example, the crop over a buried ditch will grow faster and taller because the ditch will contain additional moisture compared to the soils around it. Conversely, the buried remains of a wall, which will accelerate drainage of water, and possibly interrupt the root growth of the plants, will result in smaller, weaker crops. While most crops can produce marks, cereal crops, and wheat and barley in particular, give marks of especially good definition and resolution. The appearance of cropmarks is enhanced by dry weather when the ripening crops are short of water, and the differences in the growth of the crop can become very marked in drought conditions. From the air these ditches and pits appear as lines and dots of differently coloured crops, which represent past, and usually hidden, landscapes of the county.

Cropmarks can also be formed, in much the same manner, by geological features, however. In addition, modern agricultural practices can also leave marks and patterns which add confusion to a field containing cropmarks. Specialist interpretation of cropmark features is therefore crucial if archaeologists are to get the best information avail-able. While geological cropmarks can often mask or confuse archaeological features, they can also give useful information about the location of a prehistoric site in the natural landscape in which it existed.

The appearance of cropmarks is particularly impor-tant in Essex for a number of reasons. Almost all of the remains of prehistoric human activity have been levelled by later agriculture, unlike most upland areas where earthworks dating to the prehistoric period often survive as earthworks which can be viewed on the ground. Indeed, with around 50% of the total land-use of the county dedicated to arable cultivation, it is clear why the occurrence of cropmarks is important to archaeologists in Essex. The geology of the county also plays an important role, however, as the gravels and sands which are common along the river valleys and coastal plains, are free-draining. This results in moisture in the topsoil draining away through the gravel, unlike heavier soils, such as clay, where moisture is more likely to be retained. The greater the difference between the moisture content of the archaeological features and the surrounding soil, the more clearly defined the crop-marks are.

Over the last fifty years, the recording of cropmark sites has radically altered our understanding of the extent and complexity of archaeological landscapes in many parts of the country. Many new sites, however, continue to be discovered on an annual basis. Archaeologists must record these whenever possible as they can disappear in a matter of days, especially after heavy rain. While many sites may reappear year after year, some will appear only in the driest conditions, and many may lie under non-cereal crops which may not produce cropmarks. In addition, continual ploughing, and modern deep ploughing in particular, can erode the buried archaeological sites which cause cropmarks to form. It is important, therefore, that archaeologists continue to record from the air, not only in order to discover new sites, but also to monitor the condition of known ones. Aerial photography is a rapid and efficient method of monitoring land-use changes and other developments which may threaten archaeological deposits.

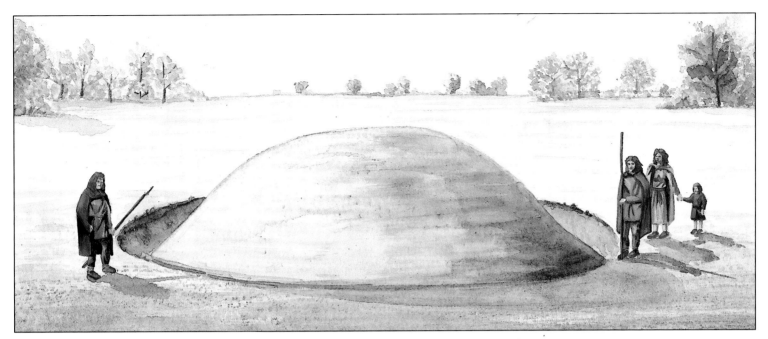

Reconstruction of a round barrow burial:
This painting depicts a round barrow, a method of burial which, although practised until the Early Medieval Period, was most common in the Bronze Age.
A circular ditch was cut and the upcast soil was used to form a mound, which would cover a burial, often a cremation placed inside a pit. Groups of barrows are often found, and these are referred to as barrow cemeteries.

How cropmarks form: This cut-away drawing illustrates the same site today, and explains how it appears as a cropmark. The ditch of the barrow has silted up over time and eventually the entire mound has become levelled by ploughing, leaving only buried remains cut into the sub-soil. Due to additional available moisture, crops growing above the buried ditch (A) and central burial pit (B) grow faster and taller and are a different colour from the crops around. The resulting circular cropmark is usually referred to by archaeologists as a **ring-ditch**, although a variety of archaeological features could produce a ring-ditch. While archaeological cropmarks can be visible on the ground, they are best understood from the air.

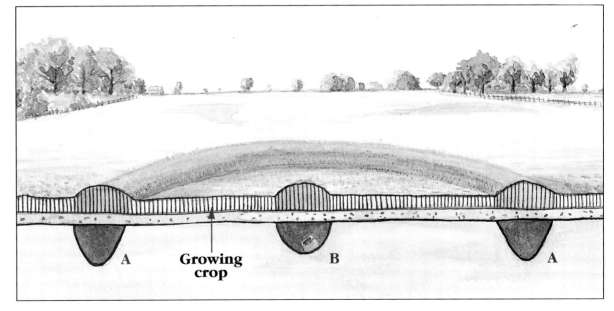

A   **Growing crop**   B   A

Interpretation and Mapping

Once archaeological features have been recorded on aerial photographs, they must be mapped in order to understand their relative shape and size. The position, shape and size of cropmarks are plotted onto modern base maps by comparing the position of 'control points' such as field boundaries and buildings, which appear both on a photograph and the relevant map. This is especially important with oblique photographs which are taken at an angle from the aircraft. The distortion of features on such photographs requires rectification in order to appreciate a site's actual shape. The resulting maps can be studied either on a site specific and therefore detailed level (large-scale), or by viewing a number of sites over a larger area of land (small-scale). This allows comparisons to be made between individual sites and provides information about the position of sites relative to each other, and the natural landscape.

Often the remains of several periods of prehistory and history are built over each other, and subsequently levelled by ploughing. In these instances, it is necessary for the interpreter to identify individual elements which are contemporary, usually on the basis of form and orientation. It is then possible to suggest how use of the landscape may have developed over time, without recourse to excavation. Interpretation of information on aerial photographs can often call upon other sources of information, such as old maps, place-names or records of artefact finds, which may suggest or support the interpretation of a particular cropmark.

The study of the morphology of cropmarks is used in order to suggest the date and function of cropmark sites with particular shared characteristics of size and shape. The many different shapes and sizes of enclosures, which appear as cropmarks, for example, can be studied and similar groups can then be compared with examples which have been excavated and which archaeologists understand. It may then be assumed that enclosures of similar size, shape and with a similar position in the landscape, might have had a similar function and be of a similar date. The distribution of these enclosures can then be studied in relation to rivers, soils and other archaeological sites in the area. The transcriptions based on aerial photographs can be seen as maps of prehistoric, Roman and medieval activity, to aid the study of the archaeology of the county. They are also used to inform archaeologists when sites are threatened by modern developments such as roads and housing.

The Archaeology Section of the County Council is currently carrying out the Essex Mapping Project, which is part of the RCHME's National Mapping Programme. The project, which in Essex began in 1993, and is funded by the RCHME, has the basic aim of mapping, at a scale of 1:10,000, archaeological and historical information visible on aerial photographs. Cropmarks, soilmarks and earthworks are mapped using set conventions, from both available vertical and specialist oblique photographs from a number of sources. Information about the morphological nature of mapped features is then compiled onto a computer database which will allow sites with similar characteristics and topographical setting to be analysed and their distributions plotted. By comparing excavated sites with groups of similar sites identified by the database, it is hoped that archaeologists will be able to understand more fully the distribution and organisation of different societies which have lived in the county in the past.

While the following chapters are arranged in a broad chronological order, it is hoped that the reader will appreciate the diversity of information which appears on the photographs, allowing a simultaneous view of both the present landscape, and relics of past activity.

Further Reading:

Glasscock, R. (ed.)
Historic Landscapes of Britain From The Air.
Cambridge University Press, 1992.

Riley, D.
Aerial Archaeology in Britain.
Shire Archaeology, 1982.

Wilson, D.
Air Photo Interpretation for Archaeologists,
Batsford, London, 1982.

Mapping cropmarks: *The photograph below shows a rectangular cropmark of a probable Iron Age enclosure (A), and geological features (B), which are the result of frost action on the subsoil during the last Ice Age. The oblique angle at which the photograph has been taken results in perspective distortion of these features however, and it is necessary to rectify the shape of the cropmarks, by plotting them onto a map, in order to fully appreciate their size and shape.*

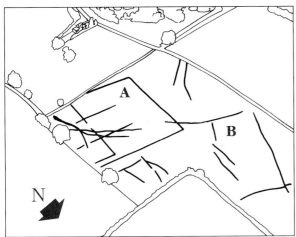

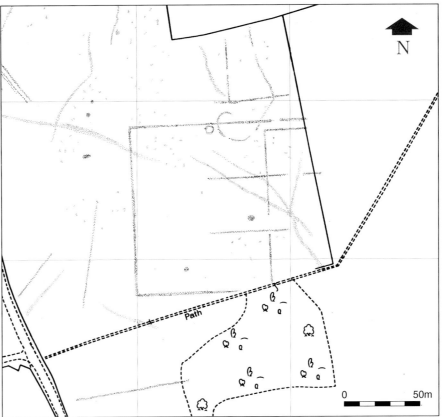

Large-scale cropmark plots *(left) at a scale of 1:2,500, allow the detailed study of the various features which appear on a photograph. Geological cropmarks (shown here in green) can be plotted to show the relationship between the archaeology and old rivers or soil variations. It also indicates areas where geological cropmarks may mask, or hide, archaeological ones. The accurate position of archaeological cropmarks (shown in red) allows archaeologists, should they need to excavate, to position trenches across features of interest. Not all archaeological features appear as cropmarks, however, and other work such as* **geophysical ground survey,** *can produce more detailed plans of sub-soil structures prior to development.*

Small-scale cropmark plots *(right), at a scale of 1:10,000, show a much larger section of the landscape, and when cropmarks (shown in red) from a number of photographs are plotted, it allows the relationship between different sites to be studied. Sites which overlap indicate that they are of different date, and the spatial distribution and orientation of sites over a large area can suggest which sites may be contemporary. It is important, however, for archaeologists to combine cropmark information with other sources, such as finds from field-walking, place-names and old maps, in order to make the most informed interpretation of how the features relate. The enclosure shown on the photograph appears at the bottom of the map (A).*

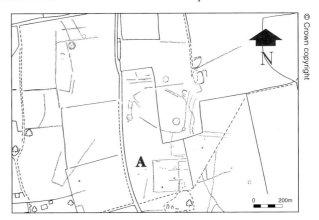

Chapter 1 The first farmers and prehistoric burial

The earliest remains of human activity in the county date from the Palaeolithic or Old Stone Age (*c.*500,000 - 10,000 BC) and the Mesolithic or Middle Stone Age (*c.*10,000 BC - *c.*4,000 BC). The economies of these early nomadic people was based on hunting, fishing and gathering of wild crops. Large, permanent structures, which would be visible from the air, were not built, and as a result archaeologists have to rely on excavations, and occasional finds of stone and flint implements, in order to create a picture of past activity.

The introduction of farming occurred in the Neolithic period, or New Stone Age (*c.*4,000 BC - *c.*2,000 BC). While in the past, the idea of the *Neolithic Revolution* saw farming as being rapidly adopted and accompanied by large-scale deforestation, it is now thought more likely that there were no sudden changes from the hunter-gatherer to farming economies. Indeed, evidence from Neolithic settlements formerly on dry land although now, due to sea level rise, in the inter-tidal zone, indicates occupation within a heavily wooded landscape. In addition it would appear that the inhabitants were at least as dependant on wild as domesticated foodstuffs. Nonetheless, forest clearance did take place and substantial, permanent structures were built. The ceremonial and funerary monuments of these early farming communities are the earliest archaeological sites which are visible from the air.

Causewayed enclosures are amongst the most striking monuments of the Neolithic period. They generally comprise one or more lines of interrupted ditch, and often cut off a small spur of land. Sites of this type are known in Essex at Springfield Lyons, near Chelmsford, and Orsett, Thurrock, where the concentric arrangement of the ditches is particularly impressive. The sites date from around 3,000 BC, although they were often used for a variety of purposes over many centuries. While the exact function of these sites is uncertain, it is probable that they related to ritual ceremonies, the exchange and trading of goods, or a combination of these.

Aerial photography in Essex has identified thirteen *long mortuary enclosures*, which appear as elongated oblong enclosures up to 60 metres long. These enclosures, by analogy with similar sites, such as long barrows, from other parts of the country, are assumed to have a burial-related function. In addition, it now seems likely that some round barrows, mounds of earth enclosed by circular ditch and containing burials, date from the Neolithic. A large, recently excavated ring-ditch at Brightlingsea was found to date from the early Neolithic, and there was some indication of funerary activity. A similar ring-ditch at West Stow, Suffolk, contained a number of cremation burials, and was found to date from the Late Neolithic. This form of burial practice was to become increasingly popular in the Bronze Age (*c.*2,000 BC - *c.*700 BC), as described below.

Perhaps one of the most unusual monuments of the Neolithic, however, are the '*cursus*' sites, of which there is one positively identified example in the county. Excavated prior to the construction of Chelmer Village, Chelmsford, the Springfield cursus consists of an elongated rectangular enclosure some 680 by 45 metres, and was found to date from around 2,500 BC. A ceremonial function, perhaps as a processional way, is usually assumed for these sites, although they may have been used as meeting places for a variety of reasons. The cursus and the nearby Springfield Lyons causewayed enclosure were in contemporary use for a number of centuries. Indeed, such impressive structures would have appeared as dominant centres in the landscape, in a similar way to the cathedrals of the Middle Ages.

Late Neolithic (*c.*2,500 - *c.*2,000 BC) ceremonial sites known as *henges* are widely distributed throughout Britain. While the name derives from Stonehenge, the sites generally consist of a large circular enclosure, often with opposing entrances. Indeed, the name 'henge' does not imply that all these sites had internal stone arrangements, or their timber equivalents. A number of possible henge, and related sites, appearing as cropmarks have been identified in Essex. Two sites, at Little Bentley and Little Bromley are possible henge sites and appear as circular, wide-ditched enclosures with opposing entrances. A third **hengiform** enclosure, at Tendring, appears to have a more unusual entrance and less substantial ditch. A suggested henge at Great Bentley, which was recently excavated, proved to be the remains of a windmill mound ditch of 13th-century date.

The Bronze Age (*c.*2,000 BC - *c.*700 BC) saw the establishment of more permanent settlements and field systems, and it is from this period that the first settlement enclosures are identifiable from the air.

The most striking of these are a number of circular ditched enclosures, dating from the Late Bronze Age (c.1,000 - c.700 BC). Five of these have now been excavated in Essex and numerous others recognised as cropmarks. An example at Springfield Lyons, Chelmsford, when excavated was found to consist of a circular, interrupted ditch with an internal palisade, and to have contained a number of timber-built round-houses. The site is immediately adjacent to the Springfield Lyons causewayed enclosure, and the form of the ditches may have emulated the earlier monument, by that time already centuries old. Similar sites have been examined at Great Baddow (Chelmsford), Ferriers Farm (Braintree) and two have been extensively excavated at Mucking, Thurrock.

In addition, rectangular settlement enclosures have been identified at Loft's Farm (Maldon) and Broomfield (Chelmsford), and may have been widely distributed across the county. It is probable, however, that there were as many unenclosed settlements at this time, as there were enclosed ones. Only the latter usually appear as cropmarks and so the cropmark evidence can distort our understanding of settlement patterns if the evidence is not viewed along with other sources such as excavation and field survey.

Burial practice in the Early and Middle Bronze Ages focused on round barrows. The funerary sites of the Bronze Age, along with the settlement evidence, seem to reflect an apparent population increase within an increasingly managed landscape. Ring-ditches (round burial mounds appearing as simple circular cropmarks) are found individually or in groups as barrow cemeteries. Large barrow cemeteries are known from Ardleigh, Chitts Hill and Brightlingsea, and, indeed, certain areas appear to have remained foci for ritual and funerary activity throughout the Neolithic and Bronze Age. An excellent example of an extensive prehistoric ritual landscape can be found along the River Stour, which forms the modern border between Essex and Suffolk.

Further Reading:

Bewley R.
Prehistoric Settlements.
Batsford, London, 1994

Darvill, T.
Prehistoric Britain.
Batsford, London, 1987.

Megaw J.V.S. and Simpson D.D.A. (eds)
Introduction to British Prehistory.
Leicester University Press, 1981.

Causewayed enclosure, Orsett, Thurrock

The outline of this enclosure, excavated in 1975 and shown to date from the Neolithic, appears as three concentric lines of interrupted ditch (A). A faint, thin line, visible just inside the outer ditches of the site, represents a trench cut to support a timber palisade. The excavations also revealed a sub-rectangular enclosure of Iron Age date (B) and confirmed that two of the small ring-ditches (C) were Saxon round barrows, around 7 metres in diameter, dating from the 7th or 8th century AD. Large, geologically formed cropmarks (D), which partly mask the archaeological features, are also visible.

It is possible that remains of the Neolithic site survived when the Iron Age enclosure was constructed. Similarly, the remains of both of these sites, and their position overlooking the lower Thames Valley, was probably a factor in the location of the Saxon cemetery. The site was discovered during aerial reconnaissance in 1973 by Cambridge University Committee for Aerial Photography.

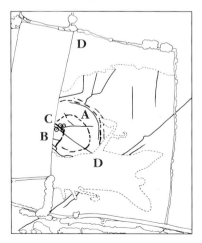

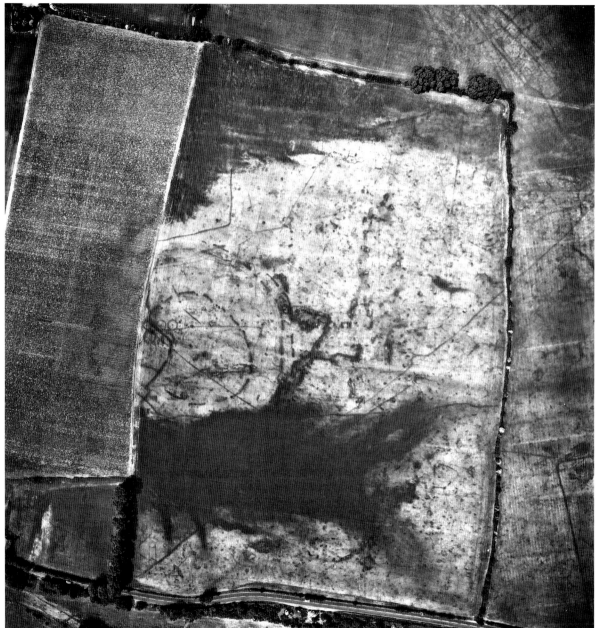

This open-ended, elongated enclosure (A) is situated on the valley floor of the river Stour in the north of the county (the river runs to the left of this photograph). The line of pits along the north-east facing ditch was first recorded on this photograph from 1996, and as yet has no parallel in the county. It is possible, however, that the lines result from quarry ditches of an earthen long barrow, and that the pits supported timber posts of a structure covered by the mound. Long barrows often contained the disarticulated skeletons of important individuals from the local Neolithic community. It seems likely that the bodies of the dead were exposed to the elements prior to internment, possibly on platforms, and it has been suggested that this would have occurred inside long mortuary enclosures. The river, which now forms the boundary between Essex and Suffolk, was the focus of an extensive prehistoric ritual landscape containing concentrations of barrows. The two ring-ditches (B) here were part of a concentrated cemetery consisting of ten barrows. Indeed, on the opposite side of the river, around 500 metres away, is the Wormingford Neolithic cursus, similar to the site at Springfield, Chelmsford (see page 13).

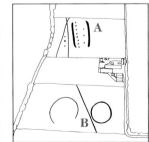

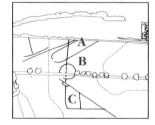

Positioned in the winding river valley of the Blackwater, this elongated enclosure (A), which is around 65 metres long, has a curved end with an entrance facing approximately south towards the river. This type of enclosure is considered to be related to elongated, or long barrows which were used as funerary monuments in the Neolithic. The circular enclosure (B) possibly represents a round barrow of around twenty-five metres in diameter. If not of contemporary construction, it was probably located beside the elongated enclosure as part of a focus for burial practice. The rectilinear features (C), however, represent the entrance of an Iron Age, or later, trackway with a small paddock constructed in one corner. The trackway again opens onto the valley floor and cuts across both the earlier enclosures indicating that they were either already levelled, or were deliberately levelled for the construction of the field boundaries.

The painting above shows this Late Neolithic ceremonial site as it may have appeared in around 2,000 BC. Evidence for both the circle of timber posts and a fire was revealed by excavation. The site is situated alongside the Chelmer river, and probably served as a meeting place for a variety of ritual and ceremonial activities, possibly involving processions, over a long period of time. The construction of such a site would have required the organised efforts of a large section of the population, and the site would have been a prestige structure and a focal point in the landscape. Indeed, it is likely that it would have remained a landmark for a considerable time after it fell out of use. The antiquarian William Stukeley gave the Latin name for a race course, 'cursus', to these structures as he assumed that they were used by ancient Britons to race chariots.

The cropmark of this elongated rectangular enclosure (A), some 700 metres long by 50 metres wide, is visible prior to excavation of the site in 1979, and subsequent destruction by residential development at Chelmer Village. Excavation at the eastern end of the cursus revealed that the ditches of the enclosure contained Neolithic pottery and flintworking debris, and that the interior of the enclosure contained numerous pits and gullies. These include a semi-circle of pits, possibly originally a circle, which would have supported upright timbers. The circle of timber posts was probably a focus of worship or ceremony, in a similar way to a stone circle. Interestingly, the nearest identified cursus at Wormingford has a circular cropmark within the enclosure at the eastern terminal. Many such sites have an east-west alignment which may suggest ritual related to sunrise and sunset. In addition to the cursus, the ditches of a possible later trackway (B) and later field boundaries (C) are visible. The dark, wide cropmark (D) results from alluvial soils relating to an ancient water-course.

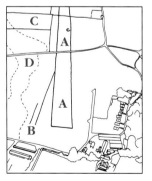

The example below appears to have a thickened ditch terminal at the north entrance, is around 30 metres in diameter and may represent a **bengiform***, or henge-related ceremonial site of the later Neolithic. The site appears to have remained a centre of activity as it is surrounded by a cropmark complex which consists of ring-ditches, enclosures and trackways of probable Iron Age date.*

This single-ditched enclosure, which has two opposing entrances, is around 40 metres in diameter and was assumed to be a henge prior to excavations in 1962 and 1971. The inner bank survived as a low mound until the 1960's and the excavations showed that this supported a post and wattle fence. Internal remains, centred around a layer of black ash, were interpreted as a small domestic structure, dated to the Late Neolithic. Finds included over 400 sherds of grooved ware pottery, 4 arrowheads and other flint artefacts, bone pins and bone fragments of pig and cattle.
In addition, Early Neolithic, pre-enclosure pottery was identified.

The site of a Neolithic settlement which, when occupied, was located in woodland on the coast of the prehistoric estuary. Sea-level rise has resulted in the site now being situated in the inter-tidal zone, where the water-logged environment preserves organic remains such as seeds and plants. The rectangular area was excavated as part of a coastal survey carried out by the Archaeology Section.

Considerable quantities of cereal grains, spikelets of emmer wheat, and hazelnut shells were found in addition to a substantial flint and ceramic assemblage. Structural remains and middens, indicating that rubbish was disposed of in specific areas, would suggest a site which was occupied on at least a semi-permanent basis. The photograph indicates that not all sources of archaeological information are visible on aerial photographs, although even in these instances they can be useful in studying the location of sites, and in monitoring changes, such as erosion, which occur there.

Above: A similar prehistoric land surface, containing scatters of flint and pottery, eroding on the mud-flats near Tollesbury.

Ring ditches at Little Clacton

The proposed route of the Clacton-Weeley bypass was found to threaten a number of archaeological features which appeared as cropmarks. These areas were examined by archaeologists who walked systematically across the fields, after ploughing, in order to collect artefacts which had been brought to the surface by the action of the plough.

The area of these two large sub-circular ring-ditches *(A)*, around twenty five metres in diameter, produced a significant cluster of flint artefacts, including twenty three struck flakes; three blade tools; and a piece of prehistoric pottery. The condition of some of the flints suggests that they were shaped, or 'knapped' nearby. The smaller ring-ditch *(B)*, being around ten metres in diameter and having a central pit, is around the average size of a round barrow, and it is possible that the larger ring-ditches represent monuments more related to the ceremonial henge sites. In addition, a number of linear features *(C)* appear to show a possible sub-rectangular enclosure, ploughed-out field boundaries, and geological features *(D)*.

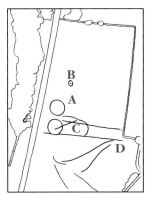

Cropmarks of a barrow cemetery (below) consisting of a number of ring-ditches of varying size, including one large double-ditched example (A) and another with a central pit (B). Elaborate barrows are known from the Early Bronze Age and, whilst few have been excavated, it is likely that many of the more complex Essex ring-ditches represent ploughed out examples of these. There is also a possible trackway (C) visible, although this may relate more to the Medieval landscape (D) than the prehistoric. The area produced a number of flint flakes and scrapers in 1926. The white building (E)

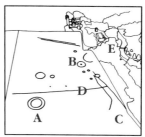

is a low lift steam pump house, dating from the 1920s, used to extract water from the river to a nearby reservoir. The pump house was built on the site of a former corn-mill.

Barrow cemetery at Dedham

A number of ring-ditches are visible here, while in previous years a further concentration was recorded in the field at the top of the frame, just above the house plot. Of particular interest is the dual concentric ring-ditch with the internal pit (A). It is possible that the perpendicular linear features (B) are later prehistoric boundaries which enclosed the barrows while they still survived as upstanding mounds, with the parallel lines forming a trackway into a more open area. Such a concentration of barrows would have been an impressive feature in the landscape, and probably would have remained a centre for burial ritual for centuries. A small gravel pit dug nearby produced a complete **collared urn** in 1914. The vessel, which was accompanied by several sherds of similar vessels, was dated to the Early Bronze Age and probably indicates the date of the cemetery. The River Stour runs close to the right of the picture, the area of pasture being former water-meadow (C).

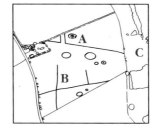

These cropmarks show the layout of an extensive prehistoric barrow cemetery, unusual in that it includes a large double-ditched barrow (A), which is around 35 metres across, and a very uncommon semi-circular feature (B). The site also contains numerous smaller ring-ditches (C), around 10 metres in diameter, which is the usual size for round barrows. The cropmarks of a probable former course of the river are also visible as a dark green mark (D) running along the line of one of the former field boundaries. This was possibly the line of the river during the prehistoric period. In addition, former field-boundaries (E) respect the area of the cemetery, suggesting that the barrows were still upstanding when the boundaries were dug. The pond (F) once functioned as a duck-decoy pond (page 64), one of the few found inland in the county. It is possible that the large ring-ditch (A) is the barrow referred to, in 1841, by the Rev. Henry Jenkins, when he describes the "large mound, in the parish of Wormingford, close to the Decoy, and the banks of the river Stour" which was "removed about six years ago, that the earth might be spread over the lower part of the field, and many hundreds of urns were then discovered, placed in parallel rows, like streets". The area has produced large quantities of worked flint, now in Colchester Museum, dating from the Neolithic period to the Bronze Age. The proximity of the cemetery to both the Wormingford cursus, on the Suffolk side of the river, and the possible long barrow shown on page 11, suggests that the cemetery may have originated as part of a Neolithic ritual landscape which continued in use into the Bronze Age. The enigmatic semi-circular feature (B) may simply show a partially completed round barrow, although the ends, or terminals, of the ditch appear to be defined by pits perhaps suggesting that the site was of a more unusual form.

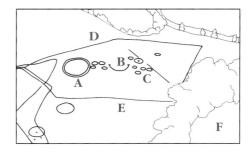

The photograph shows the buried circular ditches of twenty two barrows which resulted in cropmark formation in previous years. The top soil has been removed to allow archaeologists to excavate prior to destruction of the site by gravel extraction. Situated on the Brightlingsea peninsula of the Colne estuary, excavations proved the cemetery to consist of numerous ring-ditches, which presumably surrounded barrows, and numerous cremation

Bronze Age barrow cemetery, Brightlingsea

urns buried in pits in between the barrows. Cemeteries of this kind, with very dense clusters of ring-ditches, are characteristic of north-east Essex. A multi-period cropmark complex to the east of the cemetery may contain the remains of a related settlement site.

Above: one of the urns found during the excavation of the cemetery. The urns, containing the cremated human remains, were lowered into a pit or small grave. The scale shows 10 cm.

Bronze Age settlement at Springfield Lyons, Chelmsford

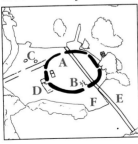

The excavations at this site, which had previously been recognised as a cropmark, revealed that the circular settlement enclosure was constructed in the Late Bronze Age. The site consisted of the circular enclosure ditch (A); a series of post-holes to support an internal rampart; a gate at the east entrance (B); a large central round-house; several smaller circular buildings and a four-post structure. It would appear that after the abandonment of the Bronze Age enclosure, activity in the area was sporadic until the Early Saxon period when a cemetery was constructed on the site (C). A total of 103 inhumation burials, largely orientated east-west, were recorded, in addition to around a hundred cremation burials. The cemetery would appear to have been partly constrained by the Bronze Age enclosure, suggesting that it remained a noticeable boundary until after the Roman period. Grave-goods associated with the inhumations included brooches, buckles, beads, pins and spearheads. The cemetery was replaced in the Later Saxon period by a settlement, possibly a farmstead, consisting of at least 13 timber buildings aligned east-west. One of these can be seen at (D). An anti-tank ditch, which formed part of a W.W.II stop line, cuts across the site (E). Newly excavated features are visible at (F).

A reconstruction of the defended enclosure as it may have appeared in around 900 BC. The construction of the site was completely of earth and timber as there was no suitable stone available locally. The round-houses depicted would have been skilfully constructed and, while it is likely that construction techniques developed over the Bronze and Iron Ages, the basic structure remained largely unaltered. It has been suggested that the multiple entrances to this site emulate the causewayed enclosures of the Neolithic, which were already ancient monuments by the Bronze Age.

The excavations show that Springfield Lyons has repeated phases of occupation, linked by sporadic activity, from the prehistoric to the early Middle Ages. It was therefore an important landmark in the area for over a thousand years.

Reconstruction of Springfield Lyons enclosure

Below: reconstruction painting of the Roman farmstead at Great Holts, Boreham, as it may have appeared in the early 4th century AD. Excavations, carried out by the Archaeology Section over two years, revealed the lay-out of the farm, including field-boundaries, trackways, ponds and farm buildings. While the field-boundaries had produced cropmarks in previous years, the central building complex had not. Water-logged conditions at the bottom of a small well yielded an assemblage of food residues, including olive stones and pine kernels from the Mediterranean, in addition to local produce such as cherries, plums and walnuts.

Above: Four gold coins, or 'staters', of Cunobelin, described by the Roman writer Suetonius as 'King of the Britons'. Cunobelin began to produce coins in around 5 AD, and the sides of the coins depicting a horse are marked 'CUN' which refers to his name. The other coins showing an ear of barley, are marked 'CAMV' for Camulodunum, the Iron Age 'capital' which became Colchester. The appearance of crops on coins of this period indicates the importance of arable farming in the economy of that time.

Chapter 2 The Trinovantes, the Romans and Saxon Essex

The Iron Age (*c.*600 BC - 43 AD) landscape which existed when the Romans arrived had developed gradually from that of the Bronze Age. It contained a larger population, resulting in increased land pressure, and more settlements. The introduction of iron transformed agriculture as metal ploughshares were produced which could break harder soils. Agricultural intensification resulted in more boundaries for land division. Deforestation, which had probably occurred gradually since the Neolithic, continued through the Iron Age and Roman periods. The fertile river valleys and coastal plains at this time were dominated by settlements of various sizes ranging from unenclosed farmsteads to villages and hamlets. Field systems and paddocks for containing animal stock were often connected to settlements by ditched trackways and drove roads. In many instances, such as at Mucking (Thurrock), there was continuity of settlement from the later Bronze Age throughout the Iron Age; in landscape terms, there was gradual evolution rather than radical change.

Society had become increasingly stratified, with chiefdoms and tribes emerging and beginning to play a more important role in society. The people of Essex during the later Iron Age went by the name *Trinovantes*, and by the time of the Roman invasion, many of the higher status individuals were already partly Romanised, as a result of increased contact and trade with the continent. The extent of development of Late Iron Age society is reflected by *Camulodunum* (Colchester), which had developed into a large settlement with its own mint, potteries, metal-workers and corn merchants. These early 'towns' are known as **oppida**, and were often situated in river valleys with an associated system of defensive dykes which radiate from them. Camulodunum also had high-status burials within enclosures at nearby Stanway. The enclosures, which were in use from the late first century BC until around 60 AD, were the burial place for members of the British nobility, one grave containing Roman pottery and a gaming board with Roman type counters.

Camulodunum was surrendered to the Romans in 43 AD, although there is little evidence, from Essex as a whole, of military sites relating to the invasion. The legionary fortress at Colchester for the XXth legion and the small fort nearby at Gosbecks are the two exceptions. The Roman army considered the south-east to have been quickly pacified and forces were moved onwards to fresh campaigns, leaving a colony of veterans at Colchester to maintain order and provide an example of Roman urban life. The Boudican rebellion of AD 61, however, saw the Trinovantes of Essex join in the uprising against Roman rule. Colchester, London and St. Albans were sacked, along with most of the smaller towns in south-east England. Once the rising had been crushed it would appear that Rome realised the need for greater supervision of the population, and Colchester was rebuilt and defended by a new town wall.

The network of Roman roads in the county has long been recognised, and was an important factor in the development of the modern landscape. Roman roads, unlike the short stretches of native trackways, were constructed along very straight lines and over long distances. Major routes were constructed from London to Chelmsford and then on to Colchester; from London to Great Dunmow; and from Colchester to Braintree and on to Braughing ('*Stane Street*'). The line of these, and many of the minor roads which criss-cross the county, often survive as modern routes, if only fragmentarily, indicating the impact which these first long distance routes have had on the development of Essex. Many of the larger Romano-British settlements, such as Braintree, Kelvedon and the recently excavated example at Heybridge, developed from existing native farmsteads and hamlets. In addition, a number of '*villas*', large agricultural estates, were constructed around the countryside. Smaller farmsteads, such as the recently excavated example at Great Holts Farm, Boreham, also appear to have been more common in the county at this time. The production of grain undoubtedly continued as an important economic factor throughout the Roman period.

Salt production was a major feature along the coast, with evidence taking the form of Red Hills, which can be found from Canvey Island, on the Thames, to Hamford Water in the north. The sites involved the extraction of salt, which was very important as a food preservative, from sea water by evaporation. There are concentrations of these sites in the Blackwater estuary, possibly related to an increase of animal husbandry, resulting in the need to preserve meat. It is possible that the success of the industry led to export of the product.

From the middle of the third century AD, the coast became subject to the threat of attack from Germanic tribes across the North Sea. In response, a series of 'Saxon Shore' forts were constructed, of which 'Othona', at Bradwell-on-Sea at the mouth of the Blackwater estuary, is an example.

The first Saxons began to arrive at the beginning of the fifth century with the decline of Roman Britain. Originally they probably arrived as raiders and then began to settle peacefully, although the classical explanation suggests that they were invited as mercenaries who then turned on their hosts. Early settlement occurred mainly along the coast and adjacent river valleys and was largely of a rural nature, although some evidence of settlement exists at Colchester. Common features of this period are the sunken-featured buildings, or *grubenhäuser*, which were timber buildings with a floor above a sunken pit for storage, and cemeteries containing both cremations and inhumations.

By the seventh century, stable kingdoms had begun to emerge and gradually the population began to adopt Christianity as their religion. Important economic, administrative and religious centres evolved at Colchester, Maldon, Witham, Newport and Waltham. Dispersed settlement was more common, however, with minster churches serving the local population.

Bede records that St. Cedd established a monastery on the site of Othona Roman fort sometime in the 650's. The existence on a nearby mud-flat of a large timber-built tidal fish-trap, recently dated by the **carbon 14** technique to the late seventh to early eighth century, might reflect an important aspect of the religious community's activities. A number of similar fish-traps have been identified around the Blackwater estuary, an example at Collin's Creek also being of Saxon date.

Further Reading:

Crummy, P.
City of Victory.
Colchester Archaeological Trust, 1997.

Cunliffe, B.
Iron Age Communities in Britain.
Routledge and Kegan Paul, London and Boston, 1991.

De La Bedoyere, G.
Roman Villas and the Countryside.
Batsford/English Heritage, 1993.

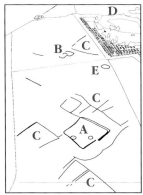

While a number of cropmark features are visible on this photograph, the line drawing indicates a large sub-rectangular enclosure (A), a further enclosure (B) and a series of related field systems (C). Enclosure (A) contains two ring-ditches, which may represent house drainage gullies, indicating a possible settlement enclosure similar to the Iron Age example excavated at Stansted Airport (see page 27). Field-systems (C), containing fields for arable cultivation and paddocks to contain animals, are laid out in a similar orientation to the enclosure, suggesting that they are of similar date. The field shown above the caravan park (D), also contains a large sub-square enclosure with a related field system on the same orientation. It would appear that this early agricultural landscape, laid out in a rectilinear pattern and orientated north-west to south-east, was already in existence prior to the building of the main Roman road from Colchester to Clacton. Excavation has shown that the field ditches in area (D) were back-filled in c.150-200 AD, although the cropmarks would also suggest that the enclosures remained in use after the road had been built. A large ring-ditch (E), of probable Bronze Age date, is also visible, indicating that this coastal plain was continually a focus of human activity throughout the prehistoric period.

25

Possible Iron Age enclosure near Farnham

The churchyard enclosure (A) of the isolated parish church near Farnham, to the north of Bishop Stortford, illustrates the scale of this possible Iron Age settlement enclosure (B), first recorded on this photograph taken in 1995. The circular ring-ditch (C) probably represents a drainage ditch around a large timber-built circular hut. A later field-boundary (D) can be seen to cut through this and the ditch of the enclosure. It is possible that Iron Age field-boundaries around the enclosure (B) influenced the layout and orientation of the Medieval field-boundaries, as has been noted in other parts of the county.

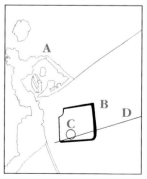

This artist's reconstruction depicts the late Iron Age 'village', of around 50 BC, which was excavated by archaeologists prior to the construction of part of the Stansted Airport complex. The circular houses are thought to be domestic, with the small central building being a possible shrine or temple. The main enclosure ditch, and buildings of such settlements, can often cause cropmarks to form, with the only other surviving features being post-holes, supporting the upright timbers of the huts, and other pits and gullies cut into the old land surface. The roughly rectangular shape of the main defensive ditch around the enclosure, has numerous parallels appearing as cropmarks in the county. While many of these may prove to be of a slightly different date, this computer generated view illustrates the general appearance of this type of enclosed settlement which was in use during the middle and late Iron Age.

Iron Age enclosure, Stansted Airport

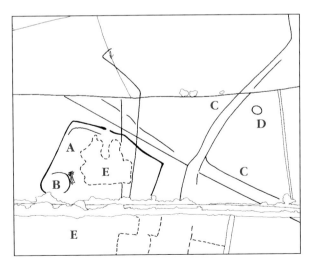

This near vertical photograph shows another such enclosure (A), which appears to have an internal feature at one corner (B) and one visible entrance. While one of the two **trackways** (C) appears to cut cross the other, it is possible that at one time there was a junction when both were in use simultaneously. Certainly the common orientation shared by the enclosures and trackway would suggest that if they were not in contemporary use, then one at least influenced the layout of the other.

An evaluation of the area, consisting of field-walking to locate finds, was carried out on the route of a proposed road and recorded a concentration of burnt flint around the enclosure in addition to a sherd of prehistoric pottery. The ring-ditch (D) may, however, indicate earlier prehistoric burial in the area. The 'marble-effect' crop-marking (E) results from ground disturbance such as quarrying, in this case it is probably a result of gravel extraction.

This oddly shaped sub-rectangular enclosure (A), is overlaid by two later features of very different origin. A later field boundary (B) crosses the enclosure and appears to have rectangular cut features (C), possibly ponds, attached to it. In addition, a World War I slit trench (D), probably cut during a training exercise, also appears as a cropmark. Defensive trenches of this type were most notoriously employed in France during W.W.I. The detail of the slit trench was first recorded during the exceptional summer of 1996.

Field-walking carried out in 1991, prior to the development of a golf course, produced a number of sherds of prehistoric pottery and worked and burnt flint. In addition, a widespread scatter of Roman tile and pottery, including *samian* ware, *mortaria* and *amphora*, dating from the 2nd to 4th centuries was recorded. Later medieval and post-medieval pottery was also located. In this instance, the additional information provided by field-walking is of little use in suggesting a date for the enclosure, and the comparison of the shape and size of the cropmark remains the most important form of evidence.

Possible Iron Age enclosure near Witham

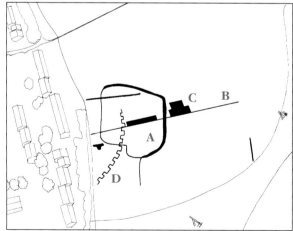

Recorded for the first time in 1996, this unusually shaped double-enclosure possibly represents a Medieval settlement form related to small castles and mottes. The orientation of the enclosure does not respect the field boundaries of the later Middle Ages, however, and as a result a prehistoric date is also possible. While there are similarities between the shape of this site and some Late Iron Age enclosures, such as the excavated example at Orsett Cock, Thurrock, there is no additional evidence, such as surface finds or maps, to confirm a date. As result, only the size and shape of the cropmark recorded on this photograph is available for study and discussion. This illustrates well the main problem faced by archaeologists who study cropmarks: a cropmark can, and often does, take a form which could have been produced by a variety of monuments covering a very large time-span. Archaeologists attempt to understand cropmarks by comparing their shape, size and position on the landscape, and this enables their interpretation of a site to be all the more informed.

This area has, in the meantime, been recorded as containing an archaeological site, probably a settlement from the Iron Age or Middle Ages, and should any development threaten the site, the opportunity will arise for archaeologists to study this shape of cropmark enclosure in detail.

The faint outline of this sub-circular enclosure (A) was again first recorded in 1996, a warm, dry summer which followed a dry winter and a long, warm summer in 1995. An entrance is visible (B) with a possible external defence, and a later field boundary (C) of probable Medieval date, is visible crossing the enclosure. The enlarged section (D) inside the enclosure possibly results from a pond which has been back-filled along with the ditch of the boundary. Both this site, and the one at High Ongar are situated on areas of heavier clay soils in the west of the county, which retain moisture and only produce cropmarks in the driest, warmest conditions. It has been assumed, due to the distribution of cropmark enclosures, that the heavier clay soils of the county were not as heavily populated in the prehistoric periods, as the lighter soils found along the rivers valleys and the coastal plains, where far more cropmarks were recorded. While this general distribution of settlement is still probably the case, it seems

likely that this distribution is exaggerated by factors affecting the production of cropmarks, and may not necessarily reflect the true picture. Indeed, this has perhaps been further complicated in that archaeologists have perhaps been less inclined to fly over these areas in the past, as they either assumed they were largely devoid of sites, or recognised that they only appeared in the very best of conditions. In recent years, the highest percentages of new sites discovered in the county have been in these areas, and it would seem likely that there are many more such enclosures on the clay soils than were previously thought, they just appear less frequently. Indeed it is possible that the long term effects of global warming and the gradually changing climate of the

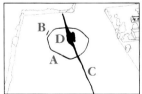

country may result in more of these sites being discovered over clay soils in the future.

This impressive series of enclosures has been excavated, prior to gravel extraction, over a number of years by the Colchester Archaeological Trust. The site originally consisted of two enclosures of the 1st century BC, which probably acted as a small settlement (A) and a stock enclosure (B) for containing domesticated animals. While one of the enclosures (B) was later re-used as a place of burial, three new enclosures (C, D and E) were built over the 1st-century AD, specifically to contain the burials of a number of important people from Camulodunum. These high-status individuals were the native aristocratic nobility, who were already highly Romanised. The subsequently named 'Warrior Burial' from enclosure (C) contained an exceptionally rich collection of grave goods. These included over twenty vessels of pottery, glass, and metal; a set of glass gaming counters and gaming board, two brooches, woollen textiles, beads, a spear, shield and a large wooden box. Dating to just after the Roman invasion, it is likely that this high-status individual enjoyed a favoured status with the new Roman authorities, and was willing to accept much of Roman culture. Excavations of enclosure (E) in 1996 produced another very rich burial which contained the almost complete remains of a gaming board with the pieces laid out ready to play. The burials are extremely important as they overlap the period of arrival of the Roman invaders and allow us to infer much about the relationship between the Romans and their native hosts.

Below: archaeological excavation, in 1992, of the burial chamber in the centre of enclosure (C).

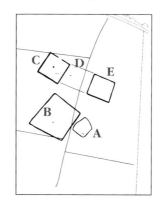

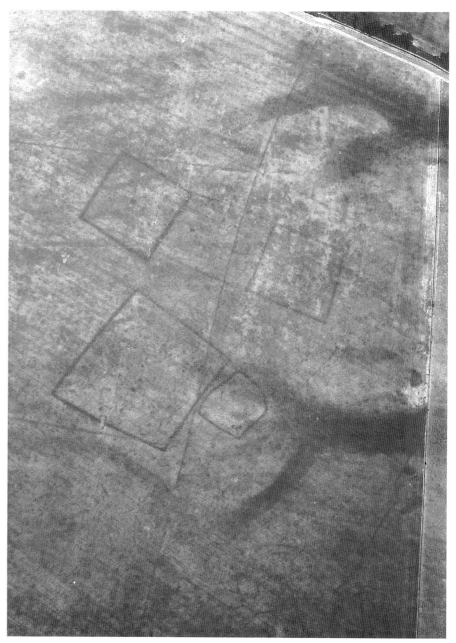

The central enclosure (A) may represent a type of late Iron Age high status burial enclosure similar to the examples which have been excavated at Stanway. While the site had been recorded as a cropmark a number of years ago, exceptional conditions in 1995 followed by the dry summer of 1996 produced a far more detailed plan of the site. This includes a slightly off-centre pit within the main enclosure (A), and another (B) just outside the smaller enclosure. The site is positioned on a flat piece of ground near a small river.

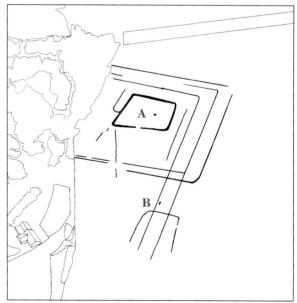

Possible burial enclosure, Uttlesford district

33

Following the Boudican revolt, Roman Colchester again flourished and the area of Gosbecks, to the south-west of the modern town, saw the construction of two major public buildings, a theatre and a temple built inside the large enclosure (A) shown here. The foundations of the temple **portico**, a walkway which was covered by a roof supported by columns, are visible. This contained a wide ditch (B) which probably served to prevent access to the temple area while allowing those in the 'portico' to look onto any ongoing ceremonies. The temple itself (C) took the form of a smaller square area within a larger one, a form commonly known as Romano-Celtic. Given that the temple is set into one corner of the sacred area of the 'portico', it is likely that the latter contained other shrines or statues, which have left little trace as they did not require such substantial foundations. The Gosbecks area developed into a thriving urban site in the Roman period which would have served as a market and entertainment centre in addition to its administrative and religious roles. The enclosure (D) is the outline of an earlier Iron Age farmstead, suggested as the farm of Cunobelin.

Below: recording the archaeological section, cut in 1997, of the main temple ditch (B).

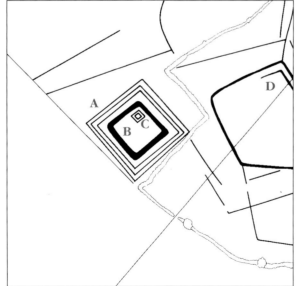

The origins of the Medieval town of Colchester lie with the conquering 30,000 strong army of Claudius, who captured Camulodunum and built the first Legionary Fortress in the country (outlined by the broken line in the drawing). The site has the classic playing-card shape of Roman military sites, and was begun in c.44 AD by Legion XX. Constructed on an east-west axis, the defences consisted of a v-shaped ditch and a rampart made of sand faced with blocks of sun-dried clay.

The fortress was deliberately placed within Camulodunum's defences but situated so as to cause minimum destruction to the existing settlement. While parts of only the barracks have been excavated so far, other ancillary buildings such as workshops, granaries, a hospital and bath-houses would also have existed. The interior of the fortress was served by compacted gravel streets, with a 'principia', a command post and administrative building in the centre.

The construction of such a site had never been seen on the British Isles before. It is possible however that the fortress was never finished as Legion XX were withdrawn to continue the invasion leaving only a colony of veterans to watch over the newly subjugated native population. The Roman town 'Colonia Victricensis' (City of the Victorious) was adapted and enlarged from the legionary fortress, with the defences being back-filled and a new street

plan being adopted. In addition, many new civic buildings were constructed including a massive Temple dedicated to Claudius and a theatre. Many of the existing fortress buildings remained in use within the extended town, however. While the town remained unwalled, a monumental arch was constructed at the western entrance (A). Boudica, queen of the Iceni, led her famous revolt around 61 AD, and stormed the town, slaughtering the inhabitants and burning the

buildings to the ground, an event which left a layer of burnt debris across the town which archaeologists can study. Soon after the revolt had been suppressed, the town was re-established and a town wall was constructed (outlined with the dark solid line), to avoid repetition of the sacking of AD 61. The wall, which survives in parts in excellent condition around the town, consisted of layers of **septaria** and mortar faced with layers of **septaria**, brick and tile. The monumental arch was incorporated into the Balkerne gate (A) as the town wall was constructed. Stone buildings, such as the temple, were renovated and the city prospered through the 2nd and 3rd centuries until its gradual decline in the

Colchester Town

late 4th century.
The layout of Medieval Colchester was substantially determined by the Roman town, with occupation in the 8th and 9th centuries being centred around surviving Roman streets. The town was restored by Edward the Elder in 917, and the 10th-century town retains much of the Roman street plan. The photograph shows the position of the castle, built over the Temple of Claudius, the largest classical temple known in Britain (B); the North gate (C); Duncans gate (D); East Gate (E); South Gate (F); and Head Gate (G).

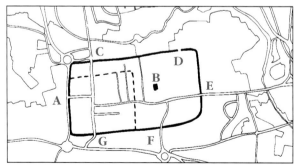

Roman road from Chelmsford to Braintree at Great Leighs

The typically straight route (the line of the modern A131) indicates that this road was originally surveyed by the Roman army when it began to construct its extensive transport system across the country. Indeed, this road runs parallel to the London to Dunmow road, around seven miles away, and is part of a larger planned system of communications.

The kink in the road in the centre of the frame (A) is where the road crosses the River Ter, indicated by the line of trees (B). Indeed, the fields at (A) have produced cropmarks which show that the Roman road continued on a straight line across the river, the road presumably being diverted during the Middle Ages. Cropmarks of Roman roads usually appear as two parallel lines, which result from drainage ditches cut on either side of the metalled surface. The undefended Roman small town of Braintree is visible in the distance (C).

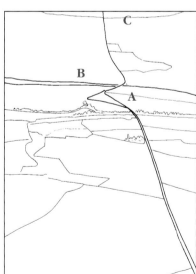

36

The wall foundations of this Roman villa (A) have resulted in **negative cropmarks**, which give a plan of the building, with its central courtyard. This type of building has numerous parallels across the country and is usually associated with larger settlement enclosures, field systems and, in high status examples, temples. Excavations to the south of the villa from 1977-1981, revealed that there had been a Middle Iron Age ditched enclosure with an internal bank, which appeared to have been enlarged and remodelled into a stock enclosure of the Late Iron Age. In addition, a group of 1st-century AD storage pits, containing carbonised grain, was discovered. These would appear to have been replaced by post-built granaries in the 2nd century AD. An Early Roman strip field-system with 23 fields, measuring around 5m x 100m was also recorded. A metalled surface running parallel to the drainage ditches of the field system was shown to post-date them, indicating re-use and development of the site over time. A small inhumation cemetery was also found, although this had been largely damaged by ploughing. It was shown to date from the later 2nd and 4th centuries AD.

An artists reconstruction of the Roman villa as it would have appeared in the late 3rd century AD. The emergence of these prestigious, partly stone-built farm estates, represents a major landscape change. They are particularly found in central and northern Essex. Many of the new villas were established and run by newly arrived immigrant officials and business entrepreneurs, and it is likely that the majority of farmsteads belonging to native farming aristocracy changed little during this period.

The use of rubble masonry in Essex villas is amongst the earliest in Britain. This allowed the construction of **hypocausts** (under floor heating systems), baths and the erection of sophisticated buildings such as the example

Cropmarks of Roman villa, Chignall St. James

at Rivenhall. The painting has been based on the interpretation of both cropmark and excavation evidence.

Red Hill, near
Tolleshunt D'Arcy

Over three hundred Red Hills, the debris from prehistoric and Roman salt making, are found along the Essex coast. Before refrigeration, salt played a crucial role in the preservation of meat and fish and was a very valuable commodity. In Essex, the sea provided a ready source of salt and many who lived along the coast would have been involved in

extracting salt from sea-water on a seasonal basis. The sun would evaporate sea-water trapped in open pans cut into the water-tight clays. This concentrated brine was then boiled, over large fires on site, in rough ceramic vessels until all the water was removed and only the salt remained.
Pieces of the crudely-made vessels, known as 'briquetage', are found in large quantities at the sites.
These pieces, together with the results of the burning process, comprise the debris which form the mounds of red soil.
This site (A) is now situated in eroding salt-marsh (B) just outside the modern sea-wall (C).
Inspection of the site on the ground (above) shows that layers of broken 'briquetage' survive above layers of charcoal, the remains of the ancient fires, used to evaporate the salt-water.

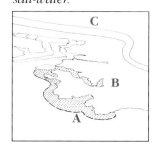

A line of Red Hills appearing as coloured soilmarks (A), indicates the prehistoric coast line, which has been reclaimed in the later Middle Ages.

The majority of these sites are now inland, due to land reclamation, and aerial photography offers a fast and accurate method of recording their position.

This photograph also indicates the destructive effect of converting reclaimed marsh (B) to arable use (see also page 65). Tradition along the coast explains that these red marks in the soil are the stains of the blood of Roman soldiers, a story which may well be very old. The continued production of sea-salt at Maldon today, however, is a reminder that the Red Hills represent the remains of an extensive salt industry which began before the invasion of the Roman army.

Red Hills on reclaimed land, Peldon

Above: pieces of the rough ceramic vessels, known as briquetage, used in the production of salt.

Othona 'Saxon Shore' fort

The outline of the Roman fort (A), known as 'Othona', is visible as a parchmark, where the stone wall foundations have caused plants growing above to become stressed in the dry summer months. 'Saxon Shore' forts were constructed in the 3rd and 4th centuries, on both sides of the English Channel, to defend the coast from Saxon raiders. The foundations of a square bastion, or turret, are visible (B), with a second cir-cular example visible at the corner (C). The plan of the fort was first recorded in 1864, when 'the foundations of two towers, one semi-circu-lar, the other horseshoe' were found. The early excavations, however, may have failed to expose the complete remains of turret B. Circular bastions at the corner, with square ones along the length of the wall are known from other forts, such as Richborough (Kent). Like most shore forts, Othona has connections with the early days of the Anglo-Saxon Church. Bede records that St. Cedd established a Christian mission, in the 650s AD, at 'Ythancester', generally accepted to be a small

town, or 'civitas', which had evolved in, or around, Othona. The Chapel of St. Peter-on-the-Wall (D and left), built on the west gate of the fort, may have replaced the original church situated somewhere inside the fort. Over half of the fort has been eroded by the advancing sea, however, and it is unlikely that much archaeology has survived under the salt-marsh (E). An anti-tank ditch (F), associated with the nearby W.W.II airfield, is visible as a dark green line cutting through the fort wall. A pill-box (G) is another indicator of defence from the last war.

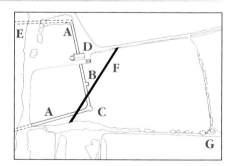

The eroded timber remains of the Sales Point fish trap (below). The line of upright timbers, which may have stood up to six feet high, would have supported a wattle facing which acted like a fence and channelled fish towards the trap area (A & B). A large concentrated deposit of fish bone exists beside one trap (A), suggesting that the collected fish were filleted on site prior to transportation. Four of these upright timbers, which were all of alder, were recently dated to the late 7th to 8th century AD. This is of interest because of its proximity to the Chapel of St. Peter-on-the-Wall (opposite), and it is possible that the site was built by the monastic settlement. The construction of the trap would have required considerable man-power and its continued use would have involved upkeep and repairs and, of course, a regular collection rota. Fish-weirs are known in many forms across the world, and have been used since the prehistoric period. These are essentially barriers of timber or stone which are designed to guide the movement of fish into nets or baskets for collection. They are often V-shaped, and positioned so that fish are channelled into the point, or 'eye', as they drift out with the falling tide. A number of large, timber-built fish-traps exist on the mud-flats of the Blackwater Estuary, and these consisted of upright posts with wattle fencing, and baskets or net traps at the 'eye'. In addition, areas of inter-woven hazel hurdling, running parallel to the upright fences may have been used as trackways to allow access to different parts of the structure. The large, roughly rectangular fish weir at Sales

Saxon tidal fish weir, Sales Point

Point, measures over three hundred metres in length and was probably designed to catch fish on both the flood (B) and ebb (A) tides. This particular fish trap is now only exposed by the lowest of tides, which often occur early in the morning as indicated by the haze caused by the sun-rise on this photograph. When in use the traps would have been exposed at all low tides, indicating sea-level rise since they were in use. Bradwell power station (C) is visible in the distance.

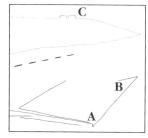

Above: an extract, showing the initial letter, from a charter of Henry VI to the Borough of Maldon in 1454. Surviving documents such as maps, deeds and charters become an increasingly important source of information for archaeologists and historians who study the Middle Ages. These two forms of evidence are often complementary and ideally both should be consulted in order to retrieve the 'overall picture' of the site, or an area, during this period.

Below: reconstruction of the medieval farm at Stebbingford, Felsted, as it may have appeared in the 13th century. As at Great Holts (page 22) only the field boundaries around the farm appeared as cropmarks, suggesting a nearby settlement. Excavated prior to road-works, the remains of three thatched buildings were uncovered. Finds included decorated ceramic jugs made in Hedingham, Ingatestone and Harlow. Arable crops were the most important produce of the farm, and would have afforded the means to pay 'tithes' to the church, rents to the landlord and food for the inhabitants and their livestock. Built in the 12th century, the site was abandoned in the mid 14th century, perhaps as a result of the Black Death of 1348.

Chapter 3 The Middle Ages

The battle of Hastings, in AD 1066, and the subsequent coronation of William of Normandy as king, saw the establishment of a new order which would rule over the region and very soon over the country as a whole. England became greatly influenced by continental Europe, and the new Norman-French aristocracy introduced a number of new types of site, which sprang up in large numbers all over the country and were to become amongst the most enduring features in the present landscape.

Castles were a key factor in the consolidation of Norman power and control over the local population. Essex has many such early castles ranging from royal strongholds such as that at Colchester, to small **motte and bailey** earthworks, which were probably built by minor nobility and occupied for only a short period. Many were occupied throughout the medieval period, however, and in some cases led to the development of closely associated towns.

The establishment of a castle at Saffron Walden resulted in settlement expansion during a period of prosperity in the twelfth and thirteenth centuries and a new town enclosure being constructed in the 1230s. Other examples, such as the great motte and bailey castle at Pleshey, however, fell into disrepair early in the post-medieval period, so that the town never outgrew its original enclosure.

Around thirty settlements could be described as towns during the medieval period in Essex. Some of these, such as Maldon, evolved from earlier urban centres. Others, such as Saffron Walden, were planted around the castles of some of the more

important medieval nobles with an eye to attracting markets, trade and profit. The development of Harwich in the fourteenth century was encouraged by the Earls of Norfolk as a purely commercial venture and the town developed trading contacts over much of continental Europe in the medieval and post-medieval periods. Aerial photography can be a valuable tool in studying the development of towns, with episodes in a settlement's development being frequently recognisable in the town's modern street plan.

Another major development in the landscape resulted from the spread of Christianity throughout England, and the growth of monasticism in the twelfth century. The eleventh to twelfth centuries saw a population increase across much of England. To cater for the spiritual needs of the rising population many new churches were built, and although often much altered over the centuries, they remain important features in the landscape and the centres of many communities.

The period saw the arrival of a number of new monastic orders from the continent. Monastic sites involved groups of individuals living and praying communally, in well organised communities which often owned large areas of land and constructed large, impressive buildings of a complexity which had rarely been seen previously in the county.

While some orders lived in isolation from the secular community, others, in addition to their regime of prayer, would provide pastoral care for the sick and infirm. St Botolph's Priory in Colchester, founded in the late eleventh century,

was the first Austin Canon's house in the country and was closely followed by establishments at St Osyth, Leez Priory and Waltham Abbey. The abbeys at Coggeshall and Tilty were Cistercian houses founded around the middle of the twelfth century. The age of the great religious houses came to an end with the dissolution of the monasteries by Henry VIII in the late 1530s, and while many of the buildings were destroyed at this time, their ground plans are often still visible from the air.

Another new class of site, the **moated homesteads**, were concentrated particularly in the eastern counties of England, with over 700 examples in Essex. Dating mainly from the thirteenth and fourteenth centuries, they usually consist of a rectangular ditch, or moat, enclosing a raised platform. The platform would have contained a house or range of buildings, and while many now appear as cropmarks, they constitute the most common class of earthwork site in the county.

Some of these remain at least partially complete and are occupied by buildings and gardens which have evolved and altered since the moat was first dug. Moated sites in Essex range from the high status King John's Hunting Lodge at Writtle, occupied over the thirteenth to early sixteenth centuries, to much smaller sites constructed by lesser gentry in the twelfth, thirteenth and fourteenth centuries. While they are distributed across the Essex landscape, the greatest concentrations are found in the north and west of the county, on the clay soils.

A number of important agricultural developments also occurred over the Middle Ages. Windmills were introduced to England at the end of the twelfth century, and were widely constructed across the county. The sites remained a common feature in Essex until the nineteenth century, and can be viewed either as upstanding buildings or as crop-marks which show their foundations.

The continued importance of farming during this period, and the need to store grain and fodder, is attested by a number of timber-framed barns, the two thirteenth-century examples at the estate of the Knights Templar, Cressing Temple, being amongst the oldest not only in England, but in Western Europe.

Perhaps one of the greatest landscape changes of this period, however, occurred along the coast. The reclamation of coastal salt-marsh involved large areas being 'inned' by the construction of sea-walls. These were then drained for use as grazing for sheep. Later, the reclaimed marsh saw the introduction of duck decoy ponds, where nets and traps were constructed to manage wildfowl. These were to become a valuable economic asset to landowners along the coast, and some remained in use until the nineteenth century.

The end of the Middle Ages also saw the development of great houses with elaborate and extensive parks and gardens. Many of these resulted from the dissolution of the great monastic sites, when the extensive church lands were confiscated from ecclesiastical landlords by the Crown, and then distributed to established estate-owning families or to favoured individuals. Leez Priory and St. Osyth Priory are prime examples of this.

The fifteenth and sixteenth centuries saw rapid improvements in the use of gunpowder and artillery which resulted in the development of new forts in the sixteenth century. Invasion being the primary threat, defence of the coast became an increasing concern, and Henry VIII first ordered a series of coastal forts and blockhouses to be constructed.

The pattern of coastal defence, for the next three hundred years, was one of short periods of construction or refurbishment, resulting directly from invasion scares, followed by longer periods of neglect. The most visually impressive of these is undoubtedly de Gomme's fort at Tilbury, which was constructed after the Dutch fleet entered the Thames estuary in 1667.

Further Reading:

Astill, G.G. and Grant, A.
The Countryside of Medieval England.
Blackwell, Oxford, 1988.

Farries, K.
Essex Windmills, Millers and Millwrights (5 vol's).
Edinburgh, 1981-8.

Kent, P.
Fortifications of East Anglia.
Lavenham, 1988.

Rackham, O.
History of the Countryside.
Weidenfeld and Nicholson, 1994.

Schofield, J and Vince, A.
Medieval Towns.
Leicester University Press, 1994.

Hubert de Burgh, Earl of Kent was granted a licence to build a castle here in 1230. The castle was constructed on a spur of land overlooking the River Thames and Canvey Island, and consisted of a strongly fortified polygonal bailey enclosed by a thick curtain wall with projecting drum towers, which are especially imposing. The site is largely ruined, partly due to subsidence caused by unsuitable geology, although the extensive layout of the site is evident. This type of castle, resulting from developments in military engineering, reached its zenith in the fortresses built by Edward I during his conquest of north Wales. Hadleigh Castle is of particular interest as it is the only work of this type in the county.

Excavations in 1971-2 revealed the remains of some of the domestic buildings, including the great hall, the foundations of which are visible to visitors today.

The castle as it would have appeared in the late 14th century after refurbishment at a cost of £2,287, by Edward III in c.1360-70. The Thames is visible in the distance beyond large expanses of marshland, indicating the dominant position that the castle held over the estuary. Edward also had a castle built at Queensborough on the south shore of the Thames.

Hedingham Castle

The castle is positioned on a spur overlooking the River Colne, in order to control access along the valley. The site consisted of a central ring-work, indicated by the oval area defined by trees and containing the **keep**. The ring-work was created by the excavation of a deep ditch which enhanced the steep scarping of the natural slopes. It had two baileys, the smaller of which is visible on the photograph above the keep. It now contains Hedingham Castle House, completed in 1719 after the estate was sold to Sir William Ashurst.

The stone-built keep was added in the first half of the 12th century, and by the 15th century, the ring-work would also have contained a range of domestic structures built of stone and timber. While the historic town of Castle Hedingham has its origins in a Saxon settlement, it owes its development as a town to the existence of the castle and patronage by the de Veres, Earls of Oxford, who were lords of the manor.

Left: the magnificent Norman keep, originally around 110 feet high, was constructed in c.1140 by Aubrey de Vere.

46

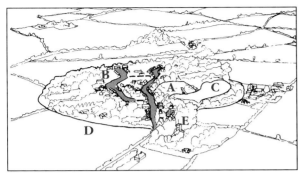

Pleshey originated with the motte (A) and bailey castle built by Geoffrey de Mandeville in the mid 12th century. The site is first mentioned as 'Plaseiz' in 1144, the name being Norman-French for enclosure. The line of the original bailey is marked by the curving line of Back Lane (B). The late 12th century saw a second phase of construction in which the southern, surviving bailey was added (C) and probably also the town enclosure (D). It is not clear whether the medieval town ever filled the town enclosure, although the post-medieval town certainly did not.

While the original chapel was constructed inside the town enclosure, in 1393 a college of canons and a new church were founded by the Duke of Gloucester, the then owner of the castle, just outside the town (E).

Pleshey

During the medieval period Pleshey was first the seat of the High Constables of England (the Mandevilles and the de Bohuns) and later part of the marriage-portion of the Queens of England. Unlike Saffron Walden, however, Pleshey was ultimately unsuccessful, and following the abandonment of the castle in the mid 16th century, it declined to village status and has grown little since. This may also have been due to the fact that it is not situated on any major route.
In the 19th century, over 70% of the inhabitants were agricultural labourers working locally.

Saffron Walden

Granted to Geoffrey de Mandeville II after the Norman Conquest, the focus of the settlement was the existing Saxon settlement of 'Waldena'. Mandeville built the castle keep (A); the inner bailey (B); the outer bailey (C) which enclosed the then town; the market (E) and possibly a parish church. The earliest reference to the castle and market is from 1141, when Walden was de Mandeville's principal holding. By the 13th century, the town had passed to the de Bohun family and in the 1230s Humphrey de Bohun laid out a large roughly rectangular town enclosure (G). Within the town enclosure ditch, known as the 'magnum fossatum', or Great Ditch, new streets were laid out in a grid pattern (H) and a new market area (F) created. The parish church of St. Mary (D) was also built on the site of the earlier market, to serve the increased population which now occupied the larger town. In the late Medieval period, Saffron Walden became a major English centre for the production of the saffron crocus (hence the name) which was used as a dye, a cooking ingredient and as a medicine. It also played an important role in the East Anglian wool industry, particularly in manufacturing cloth.

A church is recorded in Thaxted from 981 AD, and evidence for this has been unearthed from beneath the 14th to 15th-century church. The Domesday Book notes that Thaxted was a well established and prosperous settlement by the end of the Saxon period, although it is the Medieval town which is famous. The town was granted a market in 1205, and rapid expansion occurred in the 14th century as the result of a thriving cutlery industry. Poll tax returns of 1381 record that there were 79 cutlers and 11 smiths, indicating that over a third of the inhabitants were employed in the industry. It would appear that the success of the industry also attracted additional settlement.

The earlier church was rebuilt in the 14th and 15th centuries, and was probably largely funded by successful entrepreneurs. The Guild Hall was constructed at the head of Town Street in c.1450 (centre of main picture and shown below). By the 16th century, the cutlery industry had declined and weaving was introduced, with an attempt to establish a Guild of Clothiers in 1583. The layout of the core of the modern town remains largely unaltered from the medieval period.

Cistercian
Abbey, Tilty

The Abbey of St. Mary the Virgin was founded in 1153, for Cistercian monks, by Maurice FitzGeoffrey and Robert de Ferrers. The existing remains date from the late 12th century. The plan is of typical Cistercian form, and is partly visible on the ground as a series of low mounds. During dry summer months, the stone foundations cause parching of the grass covering these earth-works and the full plan of the abbey is revealed to the aerial observer.

The site was excavated in 1901 and again in 1942, and comparison of the parchmark plot and the excavation plans show that the early archaeologists failed to record a number of features, notably the buttresses in the infirmary complex (C). Tilty church (shown to the right of the frame) was once part of the extensive complex of buildings which comprised the Cistercian Abbey. The chapel, which was left for the use of the local people after the dissolution of the monasteries, was originally positioned outside the enclosure of the abbey and was intended for local people, as well as visitors and women, who were not allowed within the monastery.

Above: a computer rectified plot of the parchmarks of the Abbey. The outline of the Nave (A); Cloister Garth (B); Infirmary complex (C); Monks' Day Room (D); and Refectory (E) are all clearly visible in addition to short stretches of surviving masonry (F). The faint outline of a possible Guest House (G) is also visible. (H) is a later pond.

The Knights Templars, founded in 1118 by Hugh de Payens and nine Knights, had their headquarters on the site of Solomon's Temple in Jerusalem, hence their name. They existed to protect pilgrims to Jerusalem and defend the Holy City and were in effect warrior monks.

Cressing Temple is the earliest recorded English settlement of the Knights Templars, the manor being granted to the order by the Queen in 1137. The site passed to the rival Knights Hospitaller in 1312. In 1541 it was granted to John Smyth by Henry VIII, the family remain-ing there until 1657. The Barley barn (A and interior view) was built in c.1220. The roof, which is supported by a church-like aisled structure, was originally tiled and would have weighed over 70 tons. The Wheat barn (B), built in c.1260, is a master-piece of 'Romanesque style' carpentry and remains largely unal-tered. While the walled garden (C) appears in the style of c.1550, its origins may be earlier. Excavations have revealed some of the original layout, and on this basis, the garden has been re-designed and replanted.

Other buildings include the granary of c.1623 (D); the farmhouse of c.1618 (E); and the wagon lodge of c.1800 (F). The photograph also shows the excavations of the Templars chapel (G) and prior to the construction of the new visitors centre (H). While only the two barns remain from the medieval settlement,

Cressing Temple

excavations have suggested that settlement on the site may date as far back as the Bronze Age.

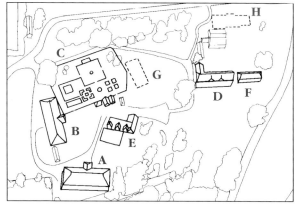

St Osyth Abbey

According to legend, St Osyth founded a nunnery at 'Cicc' (possibly meaning 'creek') in the 7th century, and while there is no current archaeological evidence to support this, Saxon finds from the town do suggest activity in the 8th to 10th centuries. The priory, which was founded in 1121 for the Austin Canons by the Bishop of London, became an Augustinian abbey in around 1200 AD. The late 15th century saw the construction of the Great Gate-house (right), which has been described as 'unexcelled by any monastic remains in the country'. In 1527, Abbot Vintoner made extensive alterations, including the building of the western range and the Bishop's lodging. The nearby town is thought to have been founded by the priory. The abbey was suppressed during the dissolution by Henry VIII in 1539, and, in 1553 was passed to Lord D'Arcy who converted some of the buildings and levelled many others, including the abbey church. In 1600 a large brick-built house was constructed on the site of the cloister, and various alterations and additions were made throughout the 18th century, when the priory grounds were landscaped. The buildings are characterised by intricate chequer-board patterning of flint, ashlar and septaria. The photograph above shows the Abbot's Tower, built by Lord D'Arcy in about 1553, on the right, and the Clock Tower on the left.

population by 1066,
existed to the south of
the area shown here.
In 1177 the secular
canons were expelled
from the priory and an
Augustinian abbey of
canons established in
1184. The monastery
became the fifth
wealthiest of the order
and due to its size and
royal patronage was
perhaps the most
important Augustinian
house in the country. It
was the last of all
English monasteries to
be dissolved.
The main features
visible here are the
abbey cloister (A); the
stone wall of the abbey
precinct (B); the abbey
forge (C); the medieval
stone bridge (D); fish-
ponds and associated
water ways (E); and a
post-medieval water
garden (F).
Legend has it that
Harold is buried
beneath a stone to the
east of the church (G).

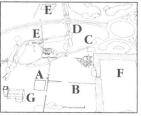

The original monastic
site was founded by
Tovi(g), a local land-
owner, for two secular
priests, and in c.1060
Harold, later King,
increased the number
of secular canons to

twelve. In 1066 Harold's
body is said to have
been buried here after
the Battle of Hastings.
Waltham Abbey has
always consisted of two
separate entities: the
abbey and the town.

The site of three pre-
Norman churches have
been identified, and
Saxon burials have
been found within the
monastic precinct. A
late Saxon village,
which had a sizeable

St. Mary the Virgin, Gt. Dunmow (below): While Domesday records a priest at Dunmow in 1066, the earliest feature at this church is the south doorway which dates to c.1280. The chancel and north and south aisles were rebuilt in c.1350, with the west tower being constructed in the first half of the 15th century. The walls are of flint rubble with limestone dressings. The immediate vicinity has produced a number of prehistoric features, including 21 worked flints, and ditches of Roman date which may represent a trackway.

St. Mary the Virgin, Great Leighs (above): The chancel, nave and tower of the church include Roman brick and tile, which may indicate nearby settlement from that date. The round tower, a rarer feature in Essex than in Suffolk or Norfolk, is Saxo-Norman in date. The west doorway is Norman. The nave was built in the 12th century, with the chancel being rebuilt in c.1330. The church was largely restored in the 19th century, and the north vestry, south porch and the spire are modern features.

Churches in the Essex countryside:
Parish churches are a very familiar part of the British landscape, and their role in the development of settlement is often underestimated. Churches usually have medieval origins and continuity of use from that period onwards makes their development as buildings often very complex. In Essex, churches are often found close to the manor house and isolated from modern settlement, as a result of the county's dispersed settlement pattern and the shifting of settlements through the centuries.

All Saint's Church, Stisted (below):
The nave north arcade is of late 12th-century date, with the south arcade and aisle being added in the early 13th century. The church also underwent much alteration in the 14th century. The present tower, which is probably on the site of an earlier one, dates from 1884, although it is likely that another tower was more conventionally placed at one end of the church in the past. The walls are of flint and pebble rubble.

Parish Churches
Stisted
Rayne

All Saint's Church, Rayne (above):
Largely rebuilt in the 19th century, apart from the west tower which is of late 15th-century date. The walls are of brick with some blue brick diaper work in the tower. The church contains features and fittings of 15th and 16th-century date, and a number of 17th-century traceried wooden panels which may be Flemish. The site is contained within the moated complex of Rayne Hall, which is visible to the left of the church. Indeed, part of the moat is visible in the foreground of the church. In addition, a number of earthworks exist between the church and the hall, including a possible fishpond.

King John's Hunting Lodge, Writtle

A reconstruction painting of the small Royal palace, built in 1211, as it may have appeared on the occasion of the visit by King Edward I and Queen Margaret in 1305. The site is one of many hunting lodges built in the great Royal Forests throughout the country, and is known to have been used by King John, Henry III and Edward I.

The site was excavated in 1955-7, and a number of internal buildings were discovered, including the hall, kitchen, chapel, gatehouse and gaol. In 1306, the estate passed to the de Bohun family, and rebuilding in the 15th century saw the early use of brick. By 1566, however, all that remained was the moat, the outer court and 'one great tyled barne and a fair large carpe pond'. A bridge across the moat, recorded on a map of 1783, was removed in 1841, and the only surviving building today is a nearby late 15th-century barn. Few of the moated homesteads of the period were of such high status as Writtle, although moated sites were status symbols indicating the class and wealth of individuals who had them built.

Takeley:
The moat of this site survives completely, although the current building is an adapted 17th-century timber-framed building built on the site of the late 13th-century timber-framed hall-house. The vegetation-covered bridge to the right of the frame is wooden and contains some very old timbers.

Good Easter:
This incomplete site appears to have been considerably altered in the recent past, containing a modern house and a landscaped moat. The site was possibly constructed by the family of Roger de la Ware, mentioned in records of 1281 and again in 1459.

Moated sites
Takeley

Good Easter

Surviving Moated Sites:

There are around 700 moated sites in the county, with a notable concentration in the west and north. This is part of a larger concentration of the site-type in south-east England. They are generally found in areas with a clay sub-soil, which prevents water from draining out of the moat, although other factors such as available land and fashion probably also dictated their distribution.

The island, or platform, of these wide-ditched enclosures would have contained a substantial house, although the buildings which survive inside them today are almost always of much later date. The moats date from around the 13th century until about 1500, although many continued in use long after that, and some remain in use today. The function of the moat was probably partly for security and defence, in much the same way as a moat around a castle, although it is also likely that moats were a status symbol, allowing local land-owners to stress their importance and advertise their wealth. Around 30% of the sites have surviving, or extant, ditches. While these have often been re-cut, extended, or otherwise altered over the years, they can often contain important environmental evidence, in the form of sediments and water-logged remains which make them archaeologically important, and sensitive, areas.

Beaumont
Otes,
Chignall

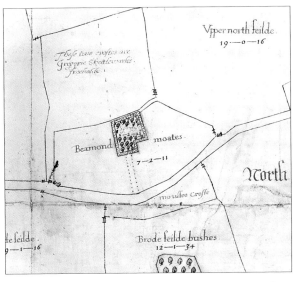

The cropmark to the right appears as 'Beamond Moates' on the John Walker the Younger map of 1599, above. The name refers to the moated homestead, and was later corrupted to 'Beaumont Otes'. It is clear from the map that by 1599 the house had disappeared, although the moat enclosure, avenue and field boundaries were still extant.

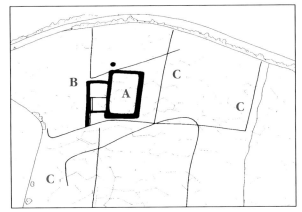

The cropmark shows very clearly the outline of a moated homestead (A), with additional features such as small annexes, which are possibly gardens and orchards (B), and associated trackways and field boundaries (C). The field has produced finds of late Medieval pottery and tile, and further research into the site revealed a map of 1599 (above left) which identified the site without doubt. While the site appeared as a faint cropmark in 1979, this photograph, taken in 1995, appears to have caught the differential growth of the plants at its optimum affording very good detail. Indeed, a network of very fine polygonal features, caused by action of frost during the last Ice Age, is also visible.

The shape and size of this cropmark, on a bend of the River Stour in the north of the county, would suggest a large moated site, with a wide, rectangular ditch with an inturned entrance (A) and an area of lighter coloured soil which may be the result of building debris (B). Another, small, sub-square enclosure is also visible (C). The site does not appear on any maps post-dating 1777. The cropmark evidence alone, however, is sufficient to suggest a settlement of probable medieval date. Some of the linear features (D) do appear as drainage ditches on later maps, and it is likely that they post-date the settlement, although their position and orientation would have been dictated by the surviving earthworks of the site at that time.

Possible Moated Site at Pentlow

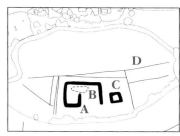

Cropmarks of a windmill, White Colne

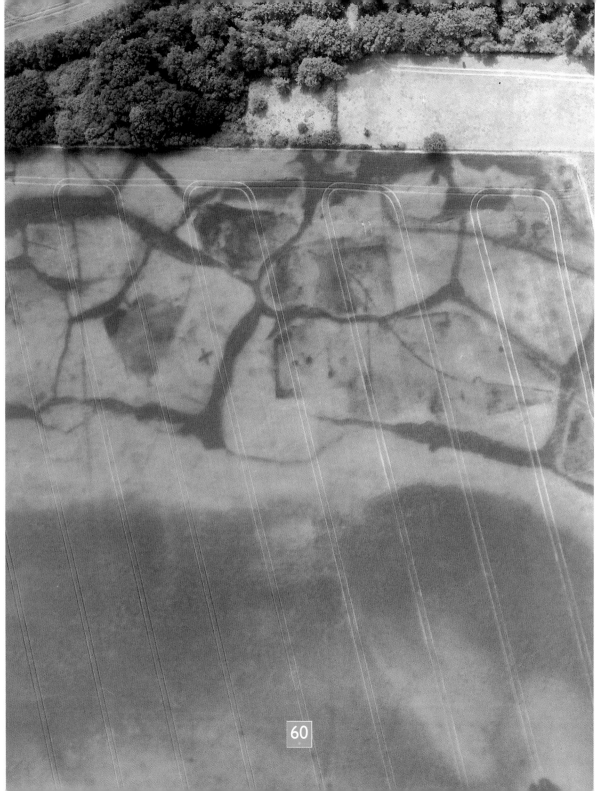

Below: the buried remains of demolished windmills often leave a recognisable cropmark formation.

The remains of a post-mill (A), cause a faint circle with a cross in the centre to appear in the crop. The cross is caused by trenches for the foundation beams of the timber mill building, which would have been supported on an upright post, giving this type of site its name. Complex geological marks (B) are the most visible features on the frame and largely mask much of the archaeology.

In addition, areas of probable former gravel extraction (C) have resulted in cropmarks, as have rectilinear marks (D) which indicate the site of a building, possibly related to the mill.

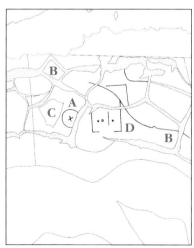

The circular feature in the centre of this frame is the remains of the earliest windmill to be excavated in the county. Prior to gravel extraction at this WWII airfield, the 18 metre wide ring-ditch was revealed to have contained a windmill mound dating from the 12th or 13th centuries. The windmill lay in the corner of a rectangular ditched enclosure, which is also visible. The cropmarks which resulted from these features led archaeologists to believe that the rectangular enclosure could be prehistoric and that the ring-ditch would have enclosed a circular building. This case shows that even experienced interpretation can be mistaken, and that ultimately, excavation is the only way of verifying the nature of the buried deposits. The vehicles pictured inside the gravel pit (top left) announce the ultimate fate of the site.

Coppice Woodland: *Coppicing is an effective way of managing a woodland in order to harvest a regular supply of wood and timber. From the prehistoric period, woodland was of major importance as a source of both fuel and building materials. The latter is especially important in Essex where there is no readily available supply of building stone. Building in prehistoric Essex was based on earthen banks and ditches, wooden fencing, and timber-built, thatched houses. The development of timber-framed buildings in the Middle Ages, which are such a characteristic part of the countryside, illustrates the importance of woodland in the county's history. In addition to timber for buildings and fuel, woodland also supplied materials for fencing, thatching and tool handles, as well as other structures, such as the Saxon fish-weirs on the coast (see page 41). The woven hurdles associated with these sites were usually made from coppiced hazel. Coppicing is based on the fact that many trees, such as ash, alder, oak, hazel, hornbeam and lime, do not die when they are cut down, but instead produce shoots from the stump from which successive crops of poles can be cut. Woodland became increasingly managed as coppice and they were often compartmentalised to allow the rotation of areas which were cut. From the Middle Ages onwards, documents and maps begin to give us far more information about how woodland was managed, and what they produced. A very valuable resource, woods were named, contained by boundaries and were privately owned. The management and exploitation of woodland, with its origins in the prehistoric, is a crucial factor in the development of the landscape, and is a tradition which has continued, albeit partially, through to the twentieth century.*

Above: *mature coppice woodland, ready to be cut back, at Chalkney Wood, near Earls Colne.*

Left: *a recently cut coppice compartment in an Essex woodland. Note the stumps, or stools, of the coppiced trees.*

During the Middle Ages, the word 'forest' indicated an area where the king, or landowner, could manage and hunt deer, rather than just an area of woodland. Indeed, the origins of Hatfield as a Forest began when deer were introduced there by Henry I in around 1100 AD. By 1215, Hatfield was one of 143 Forests in England, of which around 80 were wooded. Hatfield is broadly divided into coppices, which were surrounded by earthworks and fenced for protection, and plains, which were accessible to livestock for grazing. Eleven of the seventeen coppices survive, making-up around 50% of the forest area. The plains, which are notable for the large numbers of surviving hornbeam pollards, would have been grazed by cattle, deer, sheep, goats and horses. In addition, rabbit husbandry was carried out on at least two sites. Hatfield is the last Royal forest in England in which all the components of a medieval forest survive: deer, cattle, coppice-woods, timber trees, grass-land and fen. The forest has had a number of notable owners, including Robert the Bruce, and was acquired by the National Trust in 1924. The photograph shows areas of coppicing (A), and pollards (B), and the site of the only known surviving forest lodge (C), its present form dating to c.1590.

Hatfield Forest

Below: pollarding works on the same principle as coppicing although cutting is carried out at a height of around 3 metres to prevent browsing by livestock.

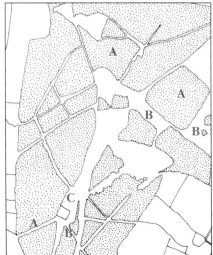

A number of these
ponds, a type intro-
duced from Holland in
the 17th century, are
found along the Essex
coast. They were used to
manage and catch
wildfowl on a commer-
cial scale and consisted
of a central pond, often
enclosed in woodland,
with a number of curved
channels, or pipes,
leading out from the
pond in different direc-
tions. The pipes were
covered by a net funnel
and a trap was built at
the end of the pipe in
which the wildfowl were
collected. In addition, a
number of wooden
screens, positioned
around the pond,

allowed the decoyman
and his dog access
around the pond with-
out alerting any feeding
birds . Wildfowl were
enticed towards the
entrance of the pipe by
the dog until the decoy-
man would appear and
frighten the ducks along
the pipe and into the
trap. Wildfowl will only
take off into the wind;
hence the reason for a
number of pipes
leading out in different
directions.
This pond has been con-
structed on the arm of
the natural creek (A) on
reclaimed grazing
marsh. It has eight pipes
(B) extending from the
central pond (C) and a
surrounding enclosure
(D). This example is not
represented on the
Chapman and André
map of 1777, although it
does appear on one of
1885, suggesting that it
was constructed at
some time in between.

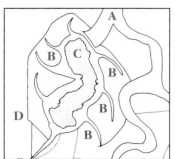

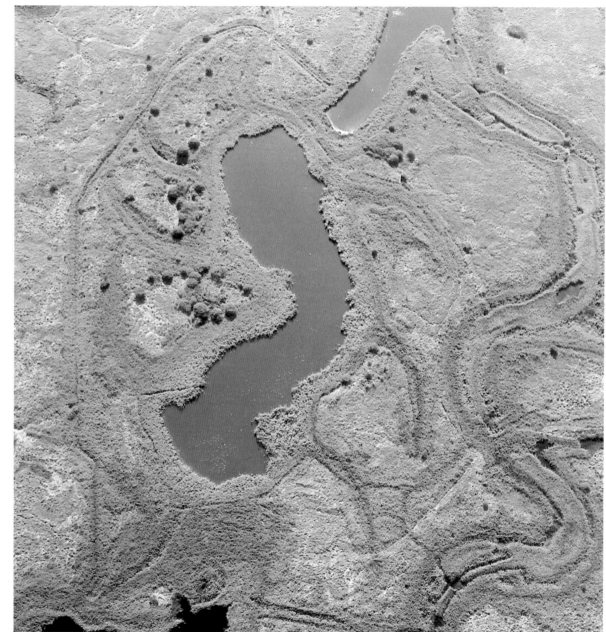

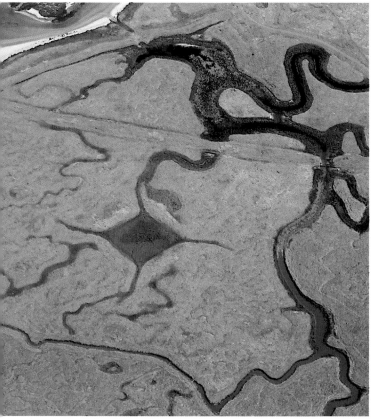

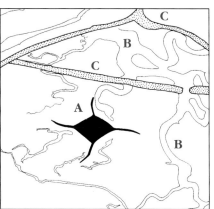

This smaller and less complex pond at Old Hall Marshes (A) is also cut into the natural creek system (B). A bank, constructed from the excavated material, can be seen to surround the pond. Numerous documents record the economic value of the ponds. In 1802 a Mr. Buxton, who owned a pond at Goldhanger, 'filled a waggon and…four stout horses were required to pull the vehicle; so many were at times caught that the lower birds in the pens were killed and pressed flat.'

The other great use of reclaimed marsh, however, was as grazing marsh for sheep. The linear banks (C) visible here relate to the reclamation, or 'inning', of the saltmarsh. While much of this process had been completed by 1598, continued drainage and upkeep would have been necessary. Indeed, Isambard Kingdom Brunel was commissioned in 1830 to install a system of iron syphons, delivered by barge, at Old Hall, to carry water out to sea.

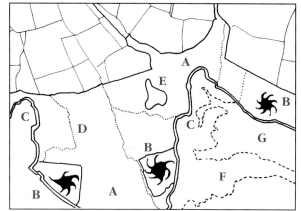

The RAF vertical photograph below shows the north bank of the Blackwater estuary as it appeared in 1947. The low angle of light casts shadow from the low relief of the dendritic creek system of the reclaimed salt-marsh (A). Three decoy ponds (B) are also visible surviving as earthworks.

The reclaimed marsh, enclosed by the modern sea-wall (C), contains a number of dykes used to 'inn' the area (D). The level enclosed area (E) is the site of a Red Hill. Beyond the sea wall, surviving mature salt-marsh (F) and mud-flats (G) are visible. Since this photograph was taken, all of the

reclaimed marsh shown has been converted to arable farming. Only the central pond survives to any degree, the example on the left being completely back-filled and the one on the right surviving only as a small circular pond. The Red Hill still appears as a soil-mark although ploughing will undoubtedly have caused damage to any archaeological levels which would have survived in 1947. Reclaimed salt-marsh is ecologically very important as an environment for rare plants, birds and insects, and all of the surviving areas have been subsequently acknowledged as important nature conservation areas.

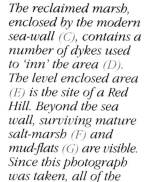

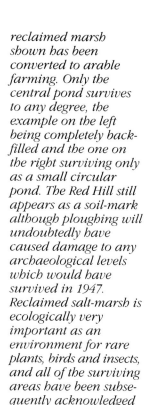

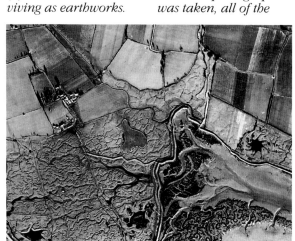

Tilbury Fort

A blockhouse was originally built here under Henry VIII, in 1539-40, as part of a nationwide system of defence against enemy fleets. This involved the forts at Tilbury and Gravesend located so as to cover the narrow river, with Coalhouse and Higham, on the Kent side, further downstream, as a first line of defence.

Late 16th-century refurbishment was accompanied by a surrounding rampart and ditch. This was replaced following the restoration of the monarchy in 1660, when Charles II ordered his chief engineer Sir Bernard de Gomme to construct a new fort. Built between 1670-82, after a number of designs had been submitted, much of the surviving defences, such as the outer glacis and inner moat, date from this period.

Various minor alter-ations and additions were carried out throughout the 18th century, including the addition of two massive powder magazines, storehouses and barracks. The fort also briefly served as a prison for Jacobite highlanders captured after the Battle of Culloden in 1746. A survey in 1793 recommended the development of an advanced fort at Coalhouse, further downstream.

During the invasion threat of the Napoleonic wars, however, ten armed hulks were manned between Tilbury and Gravesend as an additional defence. Coalhouse Fort was subsequently developed and Tilbury again became a second line of defence.

Harwich

ditch was constructed in its place on the landward side. This was possibly planned to give the most impressive show of strength to those who approached from sea. The medieval quays (C) have been shown by excavation to date from the early 14th century and to have undergone several phases of remodelling. The 'castle' (D) was really only a particularly strong tower on the town wall, again positioned for maximum show on the seaward side.

The later defensive sites of the redoubt (E) (shown on page 72) and Beacon Hill Battery (F) are also visible.

The Earls of Norfolk, who founded the town, undoubtedly recognised its position, on a peninsula at the confluence of the rivers Stour and Orwell, as a natural site for a port.

The earliest archaeological evidence for medieval settlement dates from the late 12th and early 13th cen-turies. This is supported by documentary sources which record the presence of a chapel in 1177, a market in 1222, and a charter for a market and fair in 1253. The street plan of the area of the medieval town (A), which is also shown on the oblique photograph (above) has changed very little since it was recorded on a map of 1603. The line of the town wall and ditch (B) is still partly visible through the modern layout of the town. The town received a licence to build the defences in 1338, although it took some years to complete. The wall ran up the eastern side of the town, and a bank and

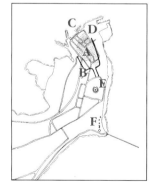

A box-scraper clearing topsoil prior to the construction of Stansted Airport in 1988. Large-scale development such as this allows archaeologists to study sites and landscapes in great detail. This project included the excavation of the settlement shown on page 27. The photograph also indicates, however, the ability of modern developments to completely alter the nature of the landscape over very large areas. Since the end of World War II, the county has seen extensive development, notably involving new housing and the construction of roads. As a result, parts of the county, which in many cases had changed little from the Middle Ages, have now been altered beyond recognition.

Chapter 4 The Recent Past and the Changing Nature of Modern Landscape

From around 1750 to the present day, there has been enormous social, economic and technological change, and these developments have resulted in extremely rapid and extensive landscape changes. In the mid eighteenth century, East Anglia was at the forefront of the so-called agricultural revolution. A number of technological innovations as well as improvements in farming methods occurred, including the enclosure of many areas of open fields. While the county has none of the heavy industries of midland and northern England, it played an important role in supplying local population centres and London with agricultural produce in the eighteenth and nineteenth centuries. A number of industries related to farming developed, including malting and brewing, with important examples at Saffron Waldon, Mistley and Coggeshall. In addition, ironworks and foundries were established to serve farming.

The introduction of turnpike roads, improvements to inland navigation, and the later introduction of railways, allowed the rapid transportation of perishable goods. Improvements to roads in the eighteenth century were accompanied by the construction of toll houses, mile posts and coaching inns. The Chelmer and Blackwater, Lea and Stort navigations also saw considerable improvements in the second half of the eighteenth century. While the development of rail services in the county was achieved by a number of small-scale companies, by 1862 these were under the control of the Great Eastern Railway, with only the London, Tilbury and Southend Railway remaining a competitor in the south. In addition to agriculture, chalk quarrying, brickearth extraction, brick manufacture, and lime production were also important industries. The coast saw extensive cultivation of oysters peaking in the mid nineteenth century, when demand from London was at its greatest. In addition, fishing and boat building employed large numbers around the coastal zone, with many coastal towns accommodating fishing fleets. The continued need for coastal defence became increasingly important in the eighteenth and nineteenth centuries, beginning with the Revolutionary and Napoleonic wars with France (1793-1815). In particular, a chain of smaller forts, called Martello towers, was constructed, between 1808 and 1812, along the Essex and Suffolk coasts from Aldeburgh to St. Osyth.

The Second World War saw the development of four major lines of defence across the county between 1940 and 1941, designed in anticipation of invasion. Coastal defences were backed by stoplines consisting of pillboxes and gun positions along rivers, or where necessary, anti-tank ditches. The Eastern Command Line ran from Mersea Island to Sudbury, the GHQ (General Headquarters) line ran from Canvey Island to Saffron Walden and the Greater London Defence Line ran around the capital in the South West of the county. In addition, numerous anti-aircraft batteries, including the so-called '**Diver**' sites, developed to counter V1 rockets, were constructed around urban areas and along the coast. Perhaps the greatest impact on the landscape, however, was the establishment of twenty two airfields by the RAF and later by the USAAF. In addition to the construction of runways with perimeter tracks and dispersal pans, they also had associated hangers, bomb dumps, technical buildings and accommodation sites, and covered large areas of land. Even when airfields have been dismantled and returned to arable use, they remain a highly visible reminder of the war.

The twentieth century saw the decline of many of the traditional industries and a shift to massive industrial development in the south of the county based on cement manufacture, power generation and oil refining. In addition, a number of explosives factories were established to supply both military and commercial users. The Royal Gunpowder Mills at Waltham Abbey, Epping Forest District, which began producing gunpowder in 1660 and continued, in the nineteenth-century, to produce guncotton and nitro-glycerine, is a site of international importance. Chelmsford and Colchester emerged as centres for electrical and mechanical engineering. The population increase of the twentieth century has resulted in residential developments around many existing settlements, the most dramatic instance being in the south of the county where overspill from London has permanently altered large areas of the countryside. Another major impact on the countryside takes the form of numerous road developments, both in the form of motorways and by-passes around urban areas.

Agriculture, which constitutes by far the most common form of land-use, has also changed radically since the second world war, with mixed arable and pasture farming becoming far more arable orientated. In addition, developing technologies have led to the grubbing out of hundreds of hedgerows (page 88) and field boundaries, which is of concern to ecologists as they are an important wildlife habitat. The removal of field boundaries, creating large open fields, has radically altered the nature of the rural landscape, which is amongst the most conservative environments in the county.

While the nature of the Essex landscape has been dramatically altered by human occupation over the last 5,000 years, the three hundred or so miles of coast in the county are also in a process of gradual change brought around by natural agents. The gradual sinking of the coast, as a result of readjustment after the last Ice Age and sea level rise, has resulted in many areas of the reclaimed marsh eroding into the sea. In addition, where sea-walls remain intact, salt-marsh, which provides important habitats for wildlife, is rapidly eroding. Sustainable management of these delicate coastal environments is now a widely acknowledged concern, and the recent experimental managed retreat site at Tollesbury, on the Blackwater estuary, may indicate

the nature of future developments in this highly dynamic landscape.

Further Reading:

Alderton, D. and Booker, J.
The Batsford Guide to the Industrial Archaeology of East Anglia.
Newton Abbot. 1980.

Bayliss, T. and Owens, S. (ed)
Britain's Changing Environment From The Air.
Cambridge University Press. 1990.

Benham, H.
Essex Gold: The fortunes of the Essex Oysterman.
Essex Record Office. 1993.

Bowyer, M.J.F.
Action Stations 1: Military Airfields of East Anglia.
Patrick Stevens Limited. 1992.

Gilman, P. and Nash, F.
Fortress Essex.
Essex County Council, Planning Department. 1995.

Coalhouse Fort, River Thames

The site contains remains of fortifications from the 16th century to W.W.II. The first artillery fortification was a small blockhouse of 1539-40, and by 1547, twenty seven cannon were on site together with a small permanent garrison. Developments after 1553 concentrated upstream at Tilbury and Gravesend, however. In 1799 a semi-circular battery was constructed with guns mounted on traversing platforms, allowing faster turning. This was abandoned after the conclusion of the Napoleonic wars in 1815. Following Lord Palmerston's recommendation to improve coastal defence in 1846, the battery was extended and enclosed inside a larger new fort with a broad water-filled ditch. The Royal Commission Fort of 1861-74, resulted from technological advances and the conclusion that the fort again would be unable to offer sufficient defence. The updated fort consisted of an arc of granite-faced gun case-mates with iron shields and an open battery to the south. The fort was manned throughout W.W.I, when an anti-aircraft battery was regularly employed to defend against German Zeppelin airships; and W.W.II, when two light anti-aircraft batteries and various other defences were added.

Below: re-enactment with 18th-century artillery.

Harwich

Clacton

Coastal defences

Harwich Redoubt

Built between 1807 and 1810, the redoubt is indicative of the particular attention the port received during the Napoleonic period. Measuring over 60 metres in diameter, the walls of the fort were 2.5 metres thick and required millions of bricks for their construction. Ten 24-pounder guns were installed on the roof above heavily protected chambers known as 'casemates', which were used to house the guns and associated equipment.

The building contained a circular parade area and was surrounded by a wide, deep, brick-faced ditch.

The site has subsequently become surrounded by housing and allotments.

Martello tower No 2, Clacton-on Sea

The name of these small coastal forts derives from a tower on Mortella Point in Corsica, which, with only three guns, repulsed two British men-of-war, with 106 guns, in 1794. The towers, which were about 9.2 metres in diameter, would have required over 700,000 bricks for their construction. Entrance would have been at first-floor level, and was reached by a ladder or drawbridge. Three 24-pounder rotating guns were mounted on the roof. Eleven such towers were built along the Essex coast. The buildings behind the tower are part of the Butlin's Holiday camp into which the site was incorporated in 1935. It then served as a water storage tower, although its degree of preservation has subsequently warranted it Scheduled Ancient Monument status.

Constructed in 1890-1, to the south of Coalhouse Fort, this battery was carefully blended into the slope of the land so as to appear invisible from a distance. The long-range guns were mounted on disappearing carriages so that they were only exposed above the parapet for a few seconds while firing; they then sank behind the parapet for reloading. Energy from the recoil was stored in a cylinder of compressed air and used to raise the gun back into position. The introduction of smokeless powder added to the idea of the battery as an invisible target. A mock attack in 1895 saw the guns of the battery fire live ammunition across the river.

East Tilbury Battery

Pewit Island
Langenhoe

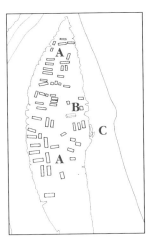

This remote salt-marsh island contains remains of the extensive oyster cultivation industry which existed along the coast. Oyster spat, of under one year, were dredged from the mud-flats and grown, for up to five years, in rectangular pits cut into the salt-marsh (A). When large enough they were packed at a timber built shed (B) and transported in sailing '**smacks**' (C). Pits are also often found cut into salt-marsh along the outside of sea-walls.

By the 19th century, large companies, such as the Colne Fishery Company and the River Roach Company, had developed in addition to individual dredgers and tenant workers. The zenith of the mid 19th century saw oysters considered as the common food of poverty-stricken Londoners.

Within decades, however, poor harvests, or spatfalls, resulted in their being regarded as an expensive delicacy. The introduction of foreign species, intended to boost production, also resulted in the introduction of new pests which became a problem. A number of reports were then published which indicated health hazards caused by oyster cultivation near sewage outfalls, and the consumption of oysters was linked to widespread outbreaks of cholera and typhoid. Oysters are now produced in the Blackwater estuary without such problems.

Above: a timber-framed oyster packing shed, built c.1890, at West Mersea. Note the line of rectangular pits in the foreground.

74

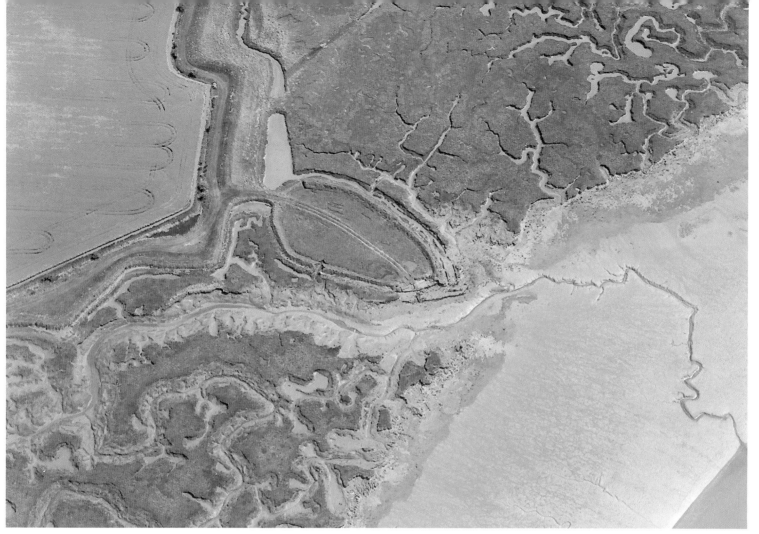

Ship's Lock
Abbott's Hall
Saltings

This unusual enclosure, constructed on mature salt-marsh to the south of Wigborough, appears on the Ordnance Survey 1st ed. map of 1881 as "Ships Lock", although no additional information about the site has been uncovered. The first and most obvious explanation is that the enclosure would have acted as a sort of dry-dock where boats were taken at high tide for repairs. The site, however, is situated in a very remote and inaccessible area of the coast which makes this explanation unlikely. A possible solution to the puzzle involves the unlikely combination of prehistoric salt and transporting Medieval sheep. It is possible that the site was originally a Red Hill, or salt-working site (see pages 38 and 39), which survived on the marsh as a mound. Indeed, a number of known examples exist nearby. Red Hills were often used by shepherds in the Middle Ages and after, for temporary occupation or as a safe resting place during a high tide. In 1607, Camden describes the Essex coast as "so low lying, that often it is all overflown, except for the higher hillocks, on which there is a safe retreat for the sheep." The hillocks referred to are presumably Red Hills. Reclaimed salt-marsh along the coast was extensively used for sheep grazing from the Middle Ages until early in this century. The arable field visible on the left of the frame was reclaimed marsh and was undoubtedly used for this purpose. It seems possible, therefore, that the name "Ships Lock" is actually a corruption of "sheeps lock" and that the site was actually constructed as a sheep pen on the existing Red Hill mound. Indeed, if the pen was used as a gathering point for sheep prior to their transportation by boat, the slippage of the name from "sheep" to "ship" might seem all the more plausible.

Hulks at Maldon Promenade

The remains of eleven hulks on the exposed mud-flat. The five larger vessels have been identified by the Spritsail Barge Research Group as the dismantled and burnt-out remains of the following Thames barges: the British Lion, a 43-ton vessel built at Rochester in 1879; the 80-ton Mamgu of London, built in 1904 as the Cawana (later becoming the Marconi Y.C. clubhouse at Heybridge); the Pretoria, a 54-ton vessel constructed at Faversham in 1902; and the William Cleverly, a 46-ton barge built at Rochester in 1899 and re-rigged in 1960's before being broken up at Maldon promenade. While the eroding hulks of wrecks are a common site on the inter-tidal mud-flats around the coast, many of these sailing craft are no longer built and many of the techniques of con-struction could be lost if they are not recorded. This is particularly important with small, regional varieties of sailing boat, such as the oyster 'smacks' of Essex, which were used by oystermen to dredge and transport oysters in the 19th century.

Maldon, at the head of the Blackwater estuary, is a scenic coastal town which, as result of its position, has been the site of human occupation since the earliest periods of prehistory. Recent excavations have revealed a significant and prosperous Late Iron Age and Romano-British settlement nearby. The town first appears in records from 913 as "Mael dun" (the hill marked with the cross), and in 916 when Edward the Elder ordered the construction of a **burh** there. The town is also famous for the battle which took place in 991 when a Viking fleet landed on the nearby Northey Island. This photograph of 'The Hythe' quayside, however, reflects a brief period of prosperity experienced in the 18th century as the result of maritime trading. Mills and warehouses were constructed along the waterfronts at the Hythe and Fullbridge, and this economic success was accompanied by large amounts of new building. Maritime trade was diverted from Maldon with the construction of the Chelmer and Blackwater Navigation Canal in 1797, however, and Maldon returned to its medieval role as a local market town.

'The Hythe'
Maldon

The eighteenth century saw the development of the idea of 'designed landscapes' associated with the new **Palladian** architecture of large country houses. These gardens and parks often contained follies relating to Roman and Greek antiquity, ponds and lakes, and artistically-grouped trees and avenues.

The shallow earthwork features (A & B) on this photograph appear on the map below from 1777, as ornamental park enclosures and avenues. (A) appears as still tree-lined on the map and contains a small building, recorded elsewhere as a 'temple folly'.

The park belonged to the estate of 'New Barrington Hall' and the map records that at that time, it was owned by a Charles Barrington Esquire.

Also of interest is the area of the Benedictine priory (C) and later church (D), founded in c. 1135 by Aubrey de Vere II. Part of the priory enclosure appears to have been re-used in the layout of the ornamental park.

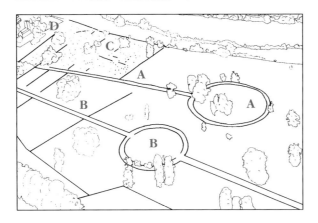

The house was designed by James Paine for Lord Petre and constructed between 1764-70. Paine, working between 1735 and 1770 was for many years the leading architect of country houses and was responsible for much of the **Palladian** influence in London. The house consists of a central rectangular porticoed Palladian palace (A) with two quadrant wings (B) connected to outer rectangular pavilion blocks of the villa style (C). The photograph shows the southern elevation with the central Corinthian podium consisting of Ionic columns sat upon five central bays. The pavilions (C) have slated roofs and chimney-stacks at bay junctions. The empty shell of the house was converted to 84 apartments in 1980.

Thorndon Hall, Brentwood

Audley End

The house was originally built between 1605 and 1614 by Thomas Howard, the 1st Earl of Suffolk, Lord Treasurer to James I. Between 1763-8, Sir John Griffin Griffin, who had inherited the house, commissioned Robert Adam to remodel the house (A), and Lancelot 'Capability' Brown to create a landscape park. While all traces of the 17th and 18th-century formal gardens were destroyed by Brown, the result was one of the finest landscaped parks in the country. The park contains a number of scattered features including the Temple of Concord (B), a small Corinthian temple built in 1790 to a design by Betlingham. Erected by Lord Howard de Walden, it commemorates King George III's recovery from his first bout of mental illness. The formal Parterre gardens (C) at the rear of the house were laid out in 1832 for the 3rd Lord Braybrooke. The gardens were completely excavated prior to restoration, allowing an accurate reconstruction to be made. Other features visible on this photograph are the river Cam (D), and the outline of Ring Hill Camp, an Iron Age hillfort (E). Preserved in the woodland, the oval enclosure, possibly of early Iron Age date, consisted of a wide, deep ditch with an internal earthen rampart. This enclosure, the defences of which were considerably strengthened by the lie of the land, would have contained an Iron Age settlement.

The wooded hillfort is one of the main views from the house, and it is likely that 'Capability' Brown was at least aware of its presence. Audley End is now in the care of English Heritage and is a popular visitor attraction. The London to Cambridge railway line is visible passing through a railway tunnel, at the top of the frame (F).

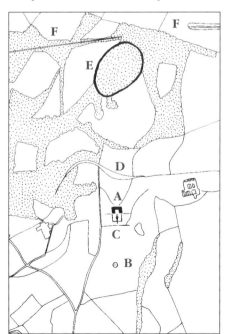

This impressive viaduct, designed by P. Bruff and completed in 1849, is built over the River Colne flood plain on the line from Marks Tey to Sudbury in South Suffolk. Constructed of yellow stock brick, with 32 arches, it was originally designed to carry two lines, although only one was ever laid. The impact of railways on the countryside was immense, with over 5,000 route miles being constructed in the country between 1840 and 1850, which was more than the existing canal system. The construction of many main lines, such as that from London to Colchester, followed the route of well established roads thereby limiting impact on the countryside. Many lesser routes such as this, however, cut across tracts of land which had remained largely unchanged since the Middle Ages.

Chappel Viaduct
Colchester

Kynochtown Explosives Factory, Thurrock

Kynochtown provides a vivid illustration of the complex, and often transient patterning left on the landscape by large-scale modern industry. Just over a century ago, the land between Shell Haven and Holehaven Creeks was low-grade agricultural land worked by Borley Farm. In the 1890s, Kynochs, a Birmingham-based ammunition manufacturers, purchased 220 acres (81ha) of land to create a large, modern explosives factory primarily to manufacture cordite for government contracts. Its remains are visible at the top of the photograph, where the protective earthen mounds or traverses which surround the potentially dangerous buildings may be seen. The many rectangular ponds in this area are borrow pits, which provided material for the mounds. Due to its isolated position, the company also created a small settlement for its key staff and named it Kynochtown after the parent firm.

The explosives factory was relatively short-lived and closed in 1919. In the 1920s the site was acquired by Cory Brothers, who established the present oil refinery on the site, which is now operated by Mobil Oil Co. Ltd. This has subsequently expanded to cover many of the remains of the explosives factory. The village of Kynochtown, later renamed Coryton, was itself swept away in 1970. Aerial photography is one of most effective methods of recording change in modern industrial plants. This RAF photograph from the 1940s shows how the site was constructed on reclaimed saltmarsh, the early phases of Shell Haven oil refinery being visible to the bottom right (see page 97).

North Site: *Gunpowder production in the area began in the 16th century, probably converting existing water-mills, although this site was certainly in use by the mid 17th century. The site was nationalised in 1787, and the 19th century saw much expansion of buildings and the complex system of canals which allowed barges to transport explosives smoothly so as to limit the risk of explosion. The site was also important for research into explosives, and many of the buildings are associated with major innovations, such as RDX which was used in the 'Dambusters' bombs, and missile propellants.*

A field survey, carried out over the 80 ha site by the RCHME in 1993, recorded in detail the remains of over three hundred years of explosives manufacture, including many of the barges remaining in silted-up canals.

English Heritage have described Waltham Abbey as "the most important site for the history of explosives in Europe", and following recent recording of the site, a heritage centre is planned.

South Site: *The shift to chemically based products in the 1880s saw the factory expand production to the South Site, with the production of gun-cotton commencing in 1890. This was soon supplemented by a nytro-glycerine factory to underpin the manufacture of cordite. Despite a disastrous explosion in 1894, many of the buildings, such as a unique nitro-glycerine wash-house, retain many internal features from the turn of the century. By the early decades of the 20th century, production of the South Site was restricted to gun cotton, which was then moved north for storage and mixing. The image shows 44 rectangular drying stoves, virtually identical in form, being surrounded on three sides by a blast con-taining earthwork. This group of widely spaced buildings (another safety measure) was connected by a canal network which linked them to the North Site. These were later replaced by tramways and then roads, all constructed on the same lines. Explosives production ceased at Waltham Abbey in 1943, although the site remained a research establishment until 1991, with research into liquid rocket fuels resulting in the conver-sion of some buildings.*

Waltham Abbey Royal Gunpowder Mills

WWI Aerodrome, Stow Maries

Land for the site was requisitioned from local farmers in 1914, although permanent brick structures were not constructed until 1918. Squadron 37 of the Royal Flying Corps was stationed here in 1916, one of three such units based in Essex with the task of defending London and East Anglia against German airships and aircraft.

By 1919, the airfield contained all three units amounting to 300 personnel, of which only 11 were pilots. The land was returned to cultivation shortly after the demise of the aerodrome in 1919, and many of the buildings subsequently served various agricultural purposes. The group of buildings represents, however, a substantially

complete W.W. I aerodrome site with over twenty surviving buildings, making it an extremely rare and well preserved monument. The surviving buildings include the Officers' Mess (A); barrack blocks for enlisted men (B); Officers' quarters (C); a water tower (D); the armoury (E); and various workshops (F).

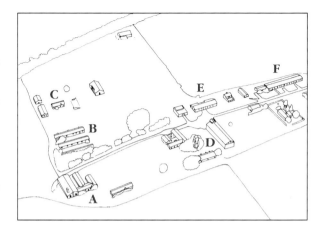

The construction of the W.W.II airfield at Earls Colne as recorded on the thirteenth of July 1942. The destructive impact on the countryside resulting from the construction of airfields is graphically illustrated here. Large areas of farmland were often compulsorily purchased and hedgerows, roads and often farm buildings were completely removed in order to allow the airfield to be built. The remains of these airfields provide valuable landmarks to aviators in the county, and even examples which have been dismantled and returned to arable farming are often visible as the modern boundaries follow the outline of the former

runways. The sites have subsequently been used for a variety of functions including golf courses and for gravel extraction (page 61).

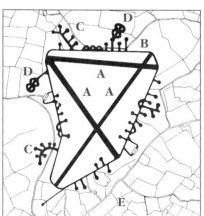

Right: The same airfield as recorded by the U.S. Airforce on 29 February 1944. Operational between 1943 and 1946, the site consists of three main runways (A) and a perimeter track (B), to which were attached a number of aircraft dispersals on which aircraft would have been kept in readiness for action. The dispersal pans began as the 'frying-pan' type (C) and evolved into the more efficient 'spectacles' loop (D), both of which can be seen on this example. The site of the bomb stores (E), which

were usually sunk into the ground, is also visible at 'Witch Wood'. Earls Colne was the first heavy bomber base to be built in Essex during W.W.II. It was the base for many of the American B-17 heavy bombers, or 'Flying Fortresses', which epitomised the USAAF presence in Essex. The northern half of the site is now used as a golf course while the southern half is an industrial park.

WWII Airfield
Earls Colne

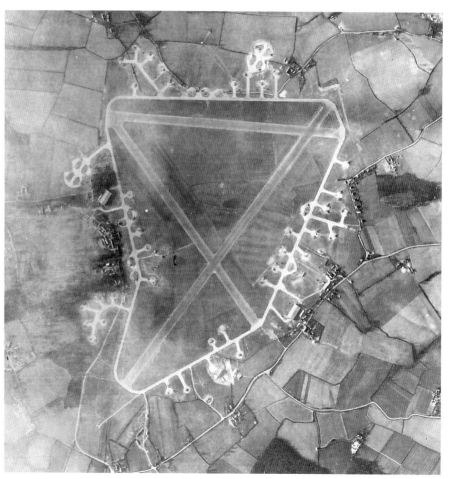

This RAF photograph, taken in February 1949, shows the remains of a large anti-aircraft battery at Broomfield, Chelmsford. Records show that in December 1943 this site was known as C13, and was manned by 373 Battery, 118 Regiment. The eight concrete gun emplacements (A), banked up with earth, can be clearly seen. The two emplacements to the bottom of the frame, which are of slightly different shape, are probably later additions to the battery. Each of these would have afforded protection, and nearby ammunition, for a 3.7" or 4.5" anti-aircraft gun. In the centre is the command post (B) which housed the predictor, height finder and plotting room. A quarry pit (C), provided earth for the construction of the banked enclosures. In addition, two small probable machine gun emplacements (D) are visible. The site has been completely dismantled since the photograph was taken and the field returned to arable farming. This indicates the importance of these early aerial photographs as a source for studying W.W.II remains. In many cases aerial photographs are the only surviving record.

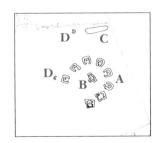

The complex coastal marsh environment to the west of Canvey Island as it appeared in January 1947. A number of former sea-walls are visible (A) which were used to reclaim the marsh, probably in the later Middle Ages; the line of the current sea-wall is clearly visible enclosing 'Corinham Marsh' on the map of 1777. The surviving system of creeks, many still water-filled, is divided into roughly equal parcels by larger natural creeks often connected by dug channels (B) to promote drainage of the marsh.

In some areas, however, these parcels of grazing marsh are sub-divided again by straight ditches, cut at right angles to each other, with small mounds of upcast soil neatly positioned along the lengths of the ditches (C). These curious features were dug during the Second World War, mainly along the coastal marshes in Essex, to interrupt the landing of enemy light aircraft which could land on the flat ground. Large areas of the marshes on the Thames, especially around Tilbury, were covered in these machine-dug defences. A scatter of bomb-craters, of unknown origin, appear in the centre of the frame (D).

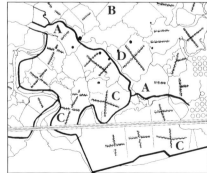

Hedgerow loss, High Easter

In Essex, much of the complex pattern of field-boundaries evolved over the Middle Ages, although the origins of the systems were sometimes older. The age of individual hedges can often be identified by the composition of species present. The orientation and patterning when viewed from the air, or on a map, can also often indicate relative date. Having evolved over hundreds of years, hedgerows become important habitats not only for plants, but also for birds, small animals and insects. Hedges also serve as a wind break, providing shelter for livestock, and protecting lighter soils which may be blown from the ploughed field. Over the last 50 years, however, the story of hedgerows has been a sad tale of drastic loss and neglect with thousands of miles of hedgerows being removed for "agricultural improvement". Hedges require regular cutting or laying (see small photo), and such maintenance is expensive compared to modern materials, such as wire fences, because of the high labour costs of what is now considered a traditional skill. Neglected hedges become lines of trees with gaps developing and the resulting hedge is then more likely to be completely removed. Latest figures suggest that the net loss of hedgerow length between 1984 and 1990 was around 21% in England, although the fact is that far more hedgerow was lost between 1950 and 1980. It has been estimated that Norfolk lost around 45% of its hedgerows between 1946-1970. Historical vertical photography, such as the RAF's National Survey of 1946-7, when compared to modern photographs, is invaluable for quantifying such figures. Post-war thinking was that larger fields were more productive and arable fields have increased in size as larger machinery has developed. Government incentives were available until the mid-

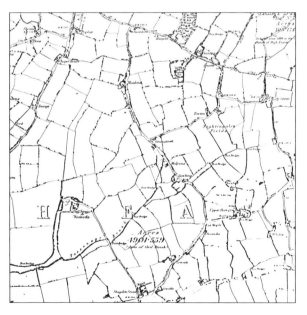

1970s for farmers to remove ancient hedgerows, particularly in East Anglia. Removing, or "grubbing" hedges involves digging out the plants and back-filling the ditch. The back-filled ditches are often visible on aerial photographs as soil-marks or cropmarks, as on the photograph above. Comparison with the Ordnance Survey first edition map of 1881 (left) indicates the hedgerows which have been removed since that date. Many of these are visible as marks on the photograph.

This settlement represents one of the last planned model villages established in England by an industrialist. Francis Crittall created a flourishing business producing metal window frames with factories at Braintree, Maldon and Witham. Growing demand, and the need for a permanent workforce, led to the purchase, in 1925, of the 220 acre Boars Tye Farm. Basing his ideas on earlier settlements at Bournville (Cadbury) and those associated with the Garden City Movement, Crittall aimed to provide high quality housing at a reasonable cost. In 1926, a ceremonial foundation stone was laid at the first house in Temple Lane and the factory (shown in the centre of the picture) became fully operational. The houses were designed by several architects with some notable examples in Silver Street being based on the International Modern Movement style. The settlement made great use of tree-lined avenues, large gardens, communal facilities and carefully planned building lines. Crittall also provided a hall, sports field, clinic, laundry, church and a store with 26 departments. By 1930 over 500 houses had been built and the settlement had a population of around 2,000 individuals. Deliberately planned settlements of this order are rare in Essex, the only other example being based around the Bata shoe factory near East Tilbury.

Silver End
Model Village

89

The origins of the town began with the construction of a few cottages, called 'Pleasant Row', in the south of Prittlewell parish in the late 18th century. These became holiday homes for wealthy individuals who enjoyed the sea air and the solitude which the area, at that time, offered. The town developed and continued to flourish as a seaside resort throughout the 19th century, although remaining independent of Prittlewell. Built in 1889, the pier, which is the longest in the UK, is 2 kilometres (over a mile) long and hosts an electric railway. It has suffered damage by storm and fire over the years, and in 1986 was broken in two when a ship collided with it. In recent years the town has developed into an active business centre, and the only County Borough until local government reorganisation in 1974. A similar status has returned as the town became a new unitary authority in 1998.

In 1959, Essex County Council initiated inquiries into the possibility of the establishment of a university in the county. In 1961 the foundation of the University of Essex was announced in the House of Commons and the County Council presented to the University the 250 acre site at Wivenhoe Park on the eastern edge of Colchester. The parklands belonged to Wivenhoe House, which was the mansion of the Rebow and Gurdon-Rebow families. The house, which dates from 1758 and was remodelled in 1846 to a new design by Thomas Hopper, is now in use as a conference centre. The first professors were appointed in 1963 and the first 122 undergraduate students were admitted in October 1964. The first new permanent buildings, designed by the University's architect C.K. Capon, were completed towards the end of autumn 1965. The number of students has continually risen over the years, 750 in 1966; 1,467 (1968); 1,943 (1970); 2,003 (1974); 2,865 (1984); 3,222 (1988); and 5,441 in 1996, with 1,374 of these being in the Graduate School. The building complex of the University has also developed and evolved over the years, with the Lecture Theatre block and Library opening in 1967, the Computer Centre opening in 1970, and the University theatre opening in 1971. The University has never grown to its projected size, however, which would have consisted of 28 residential towers (only the six visible were ever constructed) supporting 10,000 students.

University of Essex, Colchester

91

River Crouch and River Roach after the Great Flood of 1953

The 31st of January and the 1st of February 1953, saw a massive storm surge and extreme gale force winds which resulted in widespread flooding of coastal areas from north Kent to Yorkshire.

This RAF vertical photograph graphically illustrates the immense impact which the flood had along the Essex coast. The photograph shows the mouth of the River Roach, with the River Crouch to the right, Wallasea Island at the top, and Foulness Island below. Taken on the second of February 1953, the RAF's '999' series photographs record breaches in the sea-wall system. The reclaimed marsh (A) clearly remains submerged by the floodwater. The mature salt-marsh (B) and sea-walls (C) are visible above the water, indicating that the reclaimed marsh has sunk as it has dried out. Farm buildings (D) visible above the water are a reminder that over three hundred people died during the flood, and thousands were made homeless. A boat is visible entering Brankfleet on the Roach (E). Foulness is recorded as being entirely submerged by a tide in 1736, and also saw dyke-breeching in 1897.

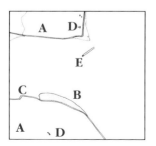

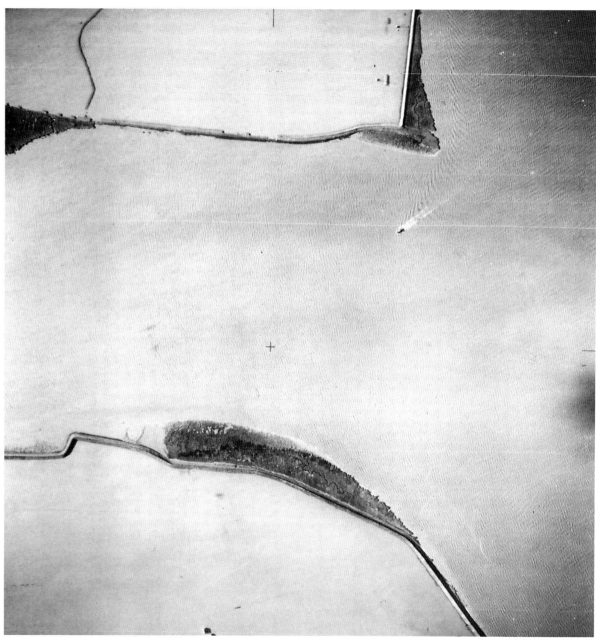

An area of 'managed retreat', which is one option for coastal management in Essex. The area enclosed by the outer sea-wall was reclaimed and used as arable land for a number of years. The wall was breached in 1995 to allow salt-marsh to regenerate on the area. Salt-marsh is a very good form of defence against erosion, as the complex systems of creeks and vegetation absorb the substantial energy contained in the tide. In addition, it is an important environment for wildlife. Salt-marsh erosion, however, is a major concern along the south-east coast, and is caused by sea-walls preventing the salt-marsh gradually retreating inland as the sea-level rises. Sea-level rise occurs because of the gradual sinking action of the south-east, caused by the removal of glacial ice-sheets after the last Ice Age. The position of this site, at the head of a large creek, has allowed estuarine silts to be quickly deposited, and this has already resulted in salt-tolerant vegetation becoming established. A number of Red Hill sites were recorded in the area; a further indication of the continuing and dynamic nature of the coast.

Coastal erosion, The Naze

The Naze at Walton is the only stretch of genuine cliff in the county, and as such is vulnerable to erosive processes which result in frequent land-slips. The exposed cliff face contains both land and sea fossils which indicate that the "red crag" deposits formed as a beach, or off-shore sand-bank, just before the onset of the ice ages. They are therefore amongst the latest geological formations in the county. The fossilised remains are as varied as whelks, rhinoceros and mammoths, perhaps the most unusual of the pre-ice age mammals to roam the county. In addition to weathering caused by the elements on the face of the cliffs, the main problem is caused by water draining down through the red crag sands and being trapped above London clay deposits. This process causes structural subsidence, slipping and instability which results in material being washed down the slope to the beach. Erosion on the cliffs is therefore often intermittent and triggered by heavy rainfall. Storm and tidal currents then carry material from the beach along the coast, often to be deposited on mud-flats, and this continual process results in the cliff face retreating inland in search of stability. While erosion at the site is often visible on an annual basis, the rate of erosion is perhaps better indicated by the fact that Walton parish church was lost to the cliff in 1798, its former site now being well below tide levels.

Breakwater,
Jaywick

The 1953 flood breached the sea-wall near Jaywick resulting in large areas of land being inundated by the surge tide. In a single night 35 people were drowned and around 600 were made homeless. Further storms in 1978 and 1983 also saw extensive areas of flooding which resulted in evacuation. The existing sea wall, built in the 1930s and improved in the 40s and 50s, had suffered badly from years of wave action from the North Sea. This has caused the shingle beaches to be washed away, lowering the beach level, and leaving increased wave energy to crash into, and over, the wall. Beach recharge was considered in the 1970s, although the technique was still in its developmental stages, and timber groynes

installed in 1972 had largely fallen into disrepair by 1984. During the 1980s it was realised that beach replenishment was a viable option, although it would require some additional defences to minimise longshore drift and the action of storm waves, which would result in the need for regular recharge. The solution was the Jaywick Sea Defence System, consisting of a combination of beach replenishment and a series of large, rock-armoured, breakwaters, one of which is visible here. Four fish-tail breakwaters, constructed from 6 to 8 tonne rocks imported from Scandinavia, were constructed along a three kilometre stretch of coast. The example shown here was completed in September 1988. The foreshore

was recharged with a marine source mixture of sand and medium gravel, raising the beach along the line of the existing seawall. This major project, only the second similar scheme to be carried out in Britain, cost £11 million between 1986 and 1988. Beach replenishment is due to be completed early in 1998, and continued surveys have shown that beach loss is minimal. The system has proved less expensive, and more environmentally acceptable, than "hard" defences such as the existing seawall, which can cost £10,000 per metre. In addition, it will provide a level of protection which would withstand the combination of high tide and wave action expected to occur only once in a 1,000 years.

Tilbury Docks
on the Thames

Archaeology has shown that the Roman port at 'Londinium' was constructed around 50 AD, and from that time on, much of London's wealth and importance resulted from the Thames and maritime trade. A plan for a dock at Tilbury first appeared in 1863. The East and West India Dock Company originated the plans for the existing docks in 1881, and by 1886 the docks had been built. When constructed the docks consisted of a tidal basin, an inner main dock with three branches, and over thirty miles of railway line. The docks were further developed by the London Port Authority in 1929, when the water area of the docks was increased and a floating double-decked jetty was constructed, allowing even the largest of ships to moor there. The success of the docks was due partly to the eastward expansion of London, based largely on developing industry, and the already established railway links. The black and white vertical photograph was taken from 6,000 feet in 1990. The oblique colour photograph below was taken from left to right across the top of the longest branch of the dock.

In the early 1920s, the Shell Oil Company constructed a refining facility on the site of the Kynochtown explosives factory. Indeed, this oblique view shows the area to the bottom right of the vertical photograph on page 82. The site, along with an additional plant for the production of lubricating oil, became known as Shell Haven. Production of oil has continued in the area, in various forms, since that time. The extensive scale of industrial plants of this nature makes the aerial view an obvious candidate for study. Machinery and equipment relating to the oil industry tends to change rapidly, and as a result, this area has seen numerous rebuilding since the once isolated marsh was first used for the production of explosives.

Shell Haven
oil refinery

97

M11/M25 Junction near Epping

Illustrating the impact of road construction on the perimeter area of London, the M25 runs from left to right across the frame at this junction with the M11 which runs north to Cambridge. In 1969 the Greater London Development Plan proposed three ringway roads around London. As a result of objections, however, a single orbital was suggested. The final section was opened in 1986 and the £1 billion, 187 km route passes through mainly Green Belt. A number of sections of the M25 have already been upgraded from three to four lanes, although all of the sections within Essex exist as three lanes and a hard shoulder. The M25 has become synonymous with traffic congestion, and there have been suggestions that the motorway should be upgraded to four lanes in each direction. While many recent road developments have been around urban areas, there continues to be a substantial impact on the countryside. Major roads sever the landscape and alter the way in which people access the countryside whether by car or on foot, the impact upon networks of public footpaths is often drastic. The majority of trips into the countryside are now made by car, with only around 5% being by public transport.

The construction of a roundabout on the A13, at Vange Mission to the south of Basildon, with the London Liverpool Street to Southend railway running along the left hand side of the frame. The impact on the landscape by such development is immediately obvious in this photograph. When such development is deemed necessary, however, as part of the overall planning procedure, archaeologists, within the Planning Department of the County Council, study the **Sites and Monuments Record** (SMR) in order to assess whether it is likely that archaeological remains will be destroyed. The SMR contains evidence from a variety of sources including old maps, stray finds, visible earthworks and aerial photographs. When it is considered likely that archaeological remains will be threatened by a development, an evaluation excavation may be carried out to assess the extent and nature of the remains. Should the remains be considered important enough, a more detailed excavation may be required to record the archaeological remains and finds on plans and photographs. The results of these excavations are then published so that others, in the future, have the opportunity to study the findings. This approach is known as 'preservation by record'.

Road construction, Basildon

Below: construction of the M11 in progress.

99

Queen Elizabeth II
Bridge, Thurrock

The first crossing of the River Thames at Dartford took the form of a 1,400 metre twin-lane bored tunnel which was opened in 1963, when traffic flows were recorded at 4 million vehicles a year. The volume of traffic steadily increased throughout the 1970s and a second tunnel, which was begun in 1972, was opened in 1980, when traffic flow was recorded at 11 million vehicles per year. In 1984, when sections of the M25 London Orbital Motorway began to be opened, it was forecast that the existing tunnels would be unable to cope with the increase in traffic by the early 1990s. As a result, work began on the bridge in 1988. The 2872 metre bridge comprises an 812 metre cable-stayed bridge and two approach viaducts, both of over 1000 metres. The piers, on which the upright pylons stand, are supported on concrete foundations which are designed to absorb impact, without sliding, from a 65,000 tonne vessel travelling at 10 knots. The 112 separate cables are arranged across the main span of the bridge in a harp configuration.

Since the bridge was opened by Her Majesty the Queen in October 1991, traffic has grown by around 40% and current forecasts project that traffic levels in excess of 40 million vehicles per year may occur in the near future, ten times the figures for 1963.

Cropmarks and Corn-circles, Wendens Ambo

This picture demonstrates the difference between cropmarks and crop-circles. A small square cropmark enclosure (A) is probably of Romano-British date, resulting from moisture in a buried ditch excavated by people living in the county some 1,800 years ago. The enclosure was first recorded on this photograph taken on July 17th 1996, a matter of days after the large multi-circular design (B) was created by people currently living in the county. The areas of flattened crop, making the design reflect the sun, gives an almost mirrored effect. While this example was visible from the M11 motorway, seen at the bottom of the frame, these crop patterns are by far best viewed from the air. Comparing the design with the electricity pylon and vehicles on the motorway will give some indication of the scale and precision involved in creating these impressive, albeit temporary, marks on the landscape.

Glossary

abbey
A type of Medieval monastic settlement which usually involved a church, cloister, chapter-house, refectory and often other buildings such as an infirmary. They were constructed for and by the main religious orders such as the Benedictines, Augustinians and Cistercians.

amphora
A large double-handled ceramic vessels used mainly to transport liquids and perishable commodities such as wine and olive oil.

anti-aircraft battery
Gun emplacements from W.W.II which were used to defend against enemy aircraft. Often arranged in a 'horse-shoe' pattern, the sites were widely distributed throughout the county.

anti-glider ditches
A W.W.II defence measure involving the construction of ditches across open areas of flat land to deter enemy aircraft from landing.

artefact
An object from the past which is studied by archaeologists and assigned a date and function. They are extremely valuable as a dating tool.

barrow cemetery
A concentrated group of round-barrows which formed a focus of burial, usually in the Bronze Age, in much the same way that a churchyard does today.

blockhouse
A type of fortification developed during the early days of artillery and found along the coast of Essex.

burgh
Anglo-Saxon settlement which was fortified in reponse to Danish invasions in the ninth and tenth centuries.

carbon-14 dating
Also known as C-14, or Radiocarbon dating, this technique gives approximate dates for organic materials by measuring surviving levels of C-14.

collared urn
A type of coarse ceramic vessel used to contain cremation remains during the Bronze Age.

Diver sites
Operation Diver began in 1944 with the aim of countering attacks from German flying-bombs. In Essex, it involved the construction of anti-aircraft and search-light batteries along the coast, many of which have subsequently been removed.

excavation
A technique whereby archaeologists dig into archaeological remains in order to record and study them. While the structures and layers are destroyed in the process, systematic photographs and plans are made which allows future generations of archaeologists the opportunity to reinterpret the records.

field-walking
A technique whereby archaeologists walk over a grid, which is laid out on a ploughed field, in order to collect stray artefacts such as flints or pottery.

flint scraper
One of a number of types of flint tool which prehistoric people used for hunting and the preparation of food and clothing.

geophysical survey
Involves a number of ground-based techniques which measure the electrical and magnetic qualities of soils, and produce plans of where features are without excavation.

grave-goods
Objects which accompany the deceased in burial, commonly jewellery, pottery and weapons.

hengiform
Enclosures which share many of the characteristics of henge monuments and assumed to be of similar date and function.

hypocaust
The Roman system of central heating whereby heat, from an external furnace, was circulated under a raised floor before escaping through flues in the wall.

keep
The central towered building of a Medieval castle, providing both living quarters and defence. The earliest examples were rectangular in plan and had an entrance on the first floor level.

moated homestead
Dating mainly to the 13th and 14th century, these consist of a central platform surrounded by a flat-bottomed ditch, or 'moat'. The enclosed area contained a domestic house and there were often associated features such as gardens or fishponds.

mortaria
Large strong bowls, with a flanged rim for gripping, which were used in the preparation of foodstuffs.

motte and bailey
The earliest castles, which were erected after the Norman Conquest. The 'motte' was a flat-topped mound which supported a tower, and the 'bailey' was an adjacent area enclosed by a ditch and containing timber buildings.

negative cropmarks
Areas of weaker crops growing above buried building foundations, roads or banks, which contain less moisture and nutrients than the surrounding soil.

oppida
Large nucleated settlements, which may have been tribal centres, of the late Iron Age. The sites often have areas demarcated by dykes (large banked and ditched boundaries) and are characterised by coinage and imported material.

Palladian
An architectural style following the principles of Andrea Palladio (1508-1580).

paddock
A field or enclosed area used to contain domesticated animals for husbandry.

pillbox
Simple W.W.II concrete defence posts commonly found around the Essex countryside. They appear either along the 'stop lines', or around airfields, towns and villages.

portico
A porch enclosed by a row of columns which supported a roof and/or pediment.

priory
Another type of monastic settlement: see Abbey.

ring-ditch
a catch-all phrase given to cropmarks of a simple circular, or sub-circular shape. They can be caused by a number of archaeological features, notably round barrows and hut-circles.

round-house
A large circular hut, constructed of timber and wattle with a thatched roofed, which was the common type of house from the Bronze Age to the Roman period in Britain. They were often surrounded by a circular drainage ditch, which can survive cut in to the sub-soil.

samian ware
Roman ceramic table-ware with a red glossy surface which was often decorated. While most of this was imported from elsewhere in the Empire, imitation varieties were made in Britain.

septaria
A low quality building stone, the only available in the county, from the Harwich area.

Sites and Monuments Record (SMR)
A list of sites of archaeological and historical importance. The Essex SMR consists of map coverage of the county with an associated computerised database, aerial photographs and reports of field-walking of sites. While SMRs are normally used within the planning process, they are usually public records which also act as a research tool.

smack
A type of small sailing craft employed for a variety of tasks, although particularly related to the oyster industry in the county. The earliest race of these vessels took place in the Blackwater estuary in 1783.

sortie
A term given by aviators to a flight.

trackway
A term used to describe prehistoric and Iron Age pathways and 'roads' which in Essex were defined by parallel ditches which often appear as cropmarks.

villa
A large and organised country estate usually associated with the Roman period in this country

wattle
A fence-like structure, made from inter-twined branches and used for a variety of uses including fencing

Acknowledgements

Thanks are primarily due to those involved with aerial survey in Essex over the years. Pete Rogers, photographer with the Planning Department of Essex County Council, has compiled a unique and valuable collection of oblique aerial views which chronicles the changing nature of the county since the early 1980s. Many of the photographs reproduced within were taken by him and his continual support and advice is hereby duly acknowledged. Dave Partridge, has piloted various archaeologists, including Caroline Ingle and Steve Wallis, over the county for the last 15 years. In addition, the navigational skills of P. J. Carter, also of the Planning Department, have proved invaluable in the busy airspace around Stansted and Luton.

I would also like to acknowledge the continued help and support of various fellow aerial archaeologists around the country, in particular Bob Bewley and Roger Featherstone, both of the RCHME, who have funded the National Mapping Programme over the last four years, and aerial reconnaissance in the county since 1984. Other 'regional flyers' and members of the Aerial Archaeology Research Group, have also been a continual source of information and advice.

Numerous colleagues within the Archaeology Section have helped with the preparation of this publication. Dave Buckley, Owen Bedwin, Paul Gilman, Maria Medlycott, Nigel Brown, Shane Gould and Pat Connell have all either provided information in some form or have read versions of the text. Particular credit is due to the Graphics Group, consisting of Iain Bell, Stewart MacNeill, Roger Massey-Ryan and Nick Nethercoat, who have prepared most of the non-photographic illustrations. Frank Gardiner has kindly allowed the reproduction of his water-colour reconstructions throughout.

Other individuals who have helped include Wayne Cocroft (RCHME); Sara Ann Kelly (ECC libraries); Steve Westover (ECC Countryside); Kevin Richell (ECC); David Andrews (ECC Historic Buildings and Design); John Clayton (Environment Agency); Ian Black (English Nature); Paul Sealey (Colchester Borough Council), and Philip Crummy (Colchester Archaeological Trust Ltd.).

Photographic and Copyright Credits

Copyright Essex County Council

Davy Strachan: page 11; 12; both photographs on page 14; ground view on page15;16; two photographs on page 17; 18; 25; 26; 28; 29; 30; 31; 33; 38; 39; aerial on page 40; ground shot on page 41; aerial on page 46; 50; 51; 53; both aerials on page 57; 58; 59; 60; 61; 64; oblique aerial on page 65; 66; 73; 74; 75; both shots on page 76; 77; 78; both shots on page 83; 84; 89; 91; 93; 95; 101.

Pete Rogers: aerial shot on page 15; two photographs on page 19; 20; 36; ground shot on page 40; aerial on page 45; ground shot on page 46; 47; both photographs on page 49; both aerials on page 52; 54; 55; 62; oblique aerial on page 67; both shots on page 71 and 72; 79; 81; 90; 94; 96; 97; 98; 99; 100.

Steve Westover: Ground shots on pages 62; 63; 88.

Steve Wallis: aerial on page 41.

Richard Havis: ground shot on page 68.

Aerofilms: Vertical aerial photographs on pages 35; 63; 67; 80; 88; 96.

Cambridge University Collection of Air Photographs: copyright reserved:

three photographs on page 3; and photographs on pages 7; 10; 13; 37; 48.

RCHME © Crown Copyright:

aerials on page 32 (NMR ref: TL9522/7/262) and page 34 (NMR ref: TL9622/5/337).

Royal Air Force © British Crown Copyright/MOD. Reproduced with permission of the Controller of Her Britannic Majesty's Stationery Office:

vertical aerial photographs on page 65; 82; both photographs on page 85; 86; 87; 92.

Copyright Colchester Museum:

studio shot on page 22.

James Fawn (copyright reserved):

studio shot on page 39.

Colchester Archaeological Trust Ltd. (copyright reserved):

ground shots on pages 32 and 34.

Other Illustrations: Copyright Credits

Frank Gardiner (copyright Essex County Council): reconstruction paintings on pages 13; 21; 37; 45; 56, 72.

Peter Froste (copyright reserved): reconstruction paintings on pages 22 and 42.

Alec Wade (copyright reserved): computer reconstruction page 27.

Based upon the Ordnance Survey mapping with the permission of the Controller of Her Majesty's Stationery Office © Crown Copyright. Unauthorised reproduction infringes Crown copyright and may lead to prosecution or civil proceedings, licence number LA 076619/97/07: 1:10,000 and 1:2,500 extracts, page 7.

Reproduced by courtesy of the Essex Record Office: Walker map, page 58: ERO ref: D/DP P6. Ordnance Survey 1st edition 6" series extract, page 88.

Reproduced by courtesy of Maldon District Council: extract of charter on page 42: ERO ref: D/B 3/13/8

Reproduced by courtesy of Phillimore and Co. Ltd: extract from Chapman and André, sheet XII on page 78.